SHE-SHED COLORING BOOK 3 INTERESTING SIGHTS

OTHER BOOKS BY REBECCA RAE

SHE-SHED FLORAL DREAMS 1
SHE-SHED FLORAL DREAMS 2
SHE-SHED TROPICAL DREAMS 1
SHE-SHED PLACES DREAMS
SHE-SHED COLORING BOOK 1
SHE-SHED COLORING BOOK 2
SHE-SHED COLORING BOOK 4
SHE-SHED COLORING BOOK 5
LITTLE RUNNING WOLF GIRL
MAN CAVE MANIA
ROYAL ANIMAL KINGDOMS OF AFRICA
ROYAL ANIMAL KINGDOMS OF ASIA
ROYAL ANIMAL KINGDOMS OF AUSTRALIA
ROYAL ANIMAL KINGDOMS OF EUROPE
ROYAL ANIMAL KINGDOMS OF NORTH AMERICA
ROYAL ANIMAL KINGDOMS OF SOUTH AMERICA
ROYAL ANIMAL KINGDOMS OF THE OCEANS AND WATERWAYS
FLIGHTS OF FANCY
A MIX OF ROYAL ANIMAL KINGDOMS

Co-Authored by Rebecca Rae
COOPER'S VIDEO QUEST
CHARLIE AND HIS WARRIOR FRIENDS

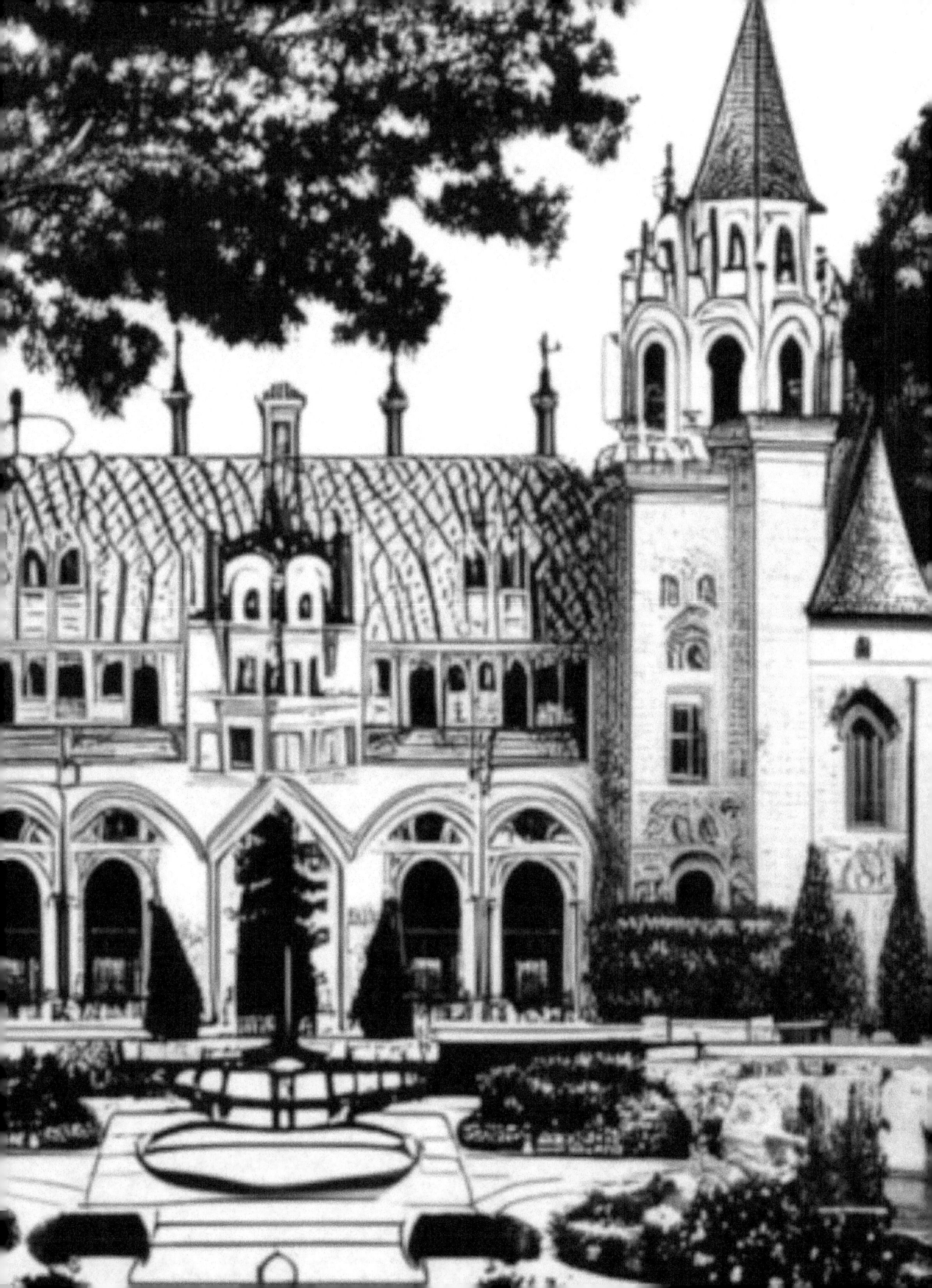

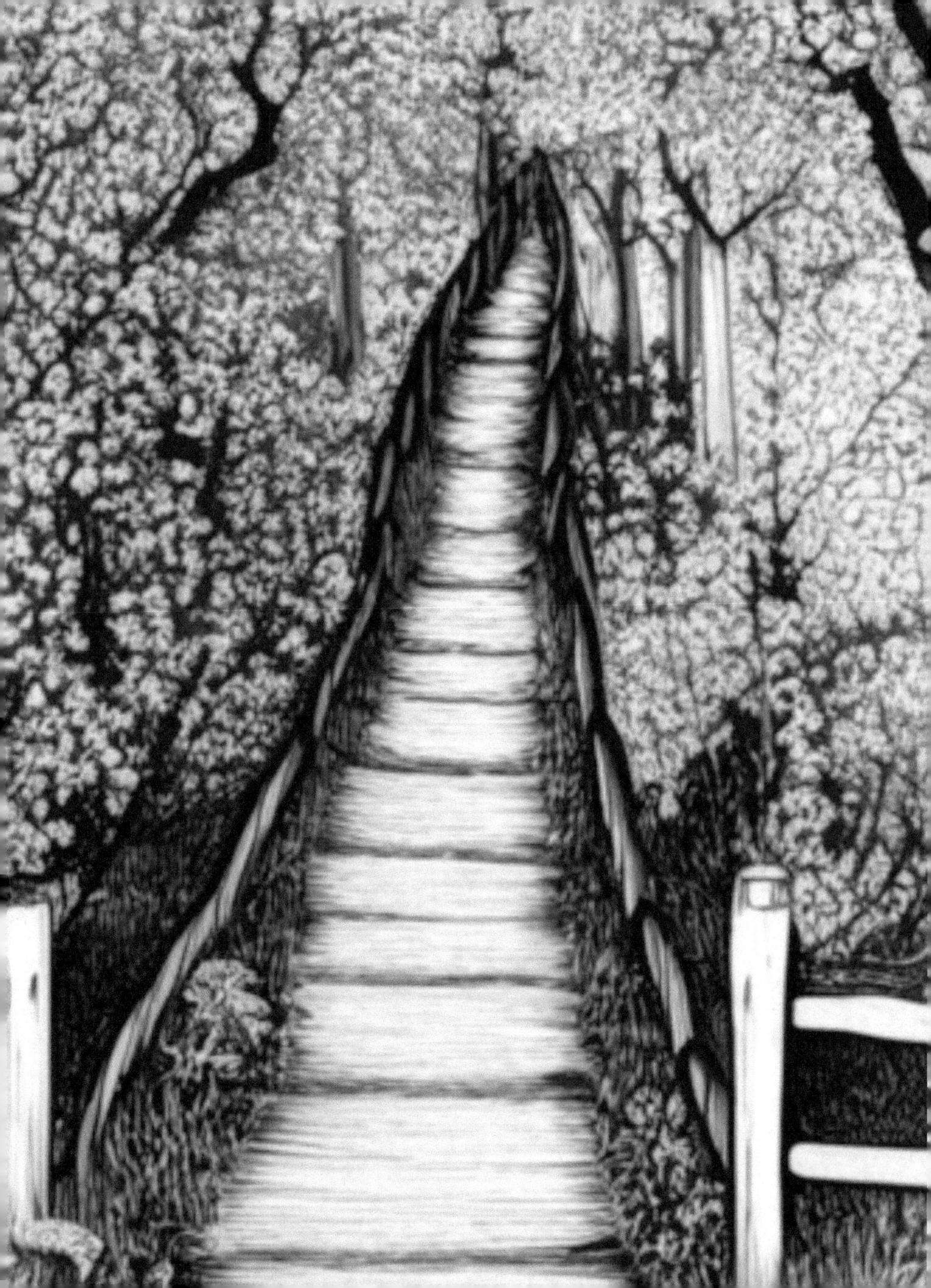

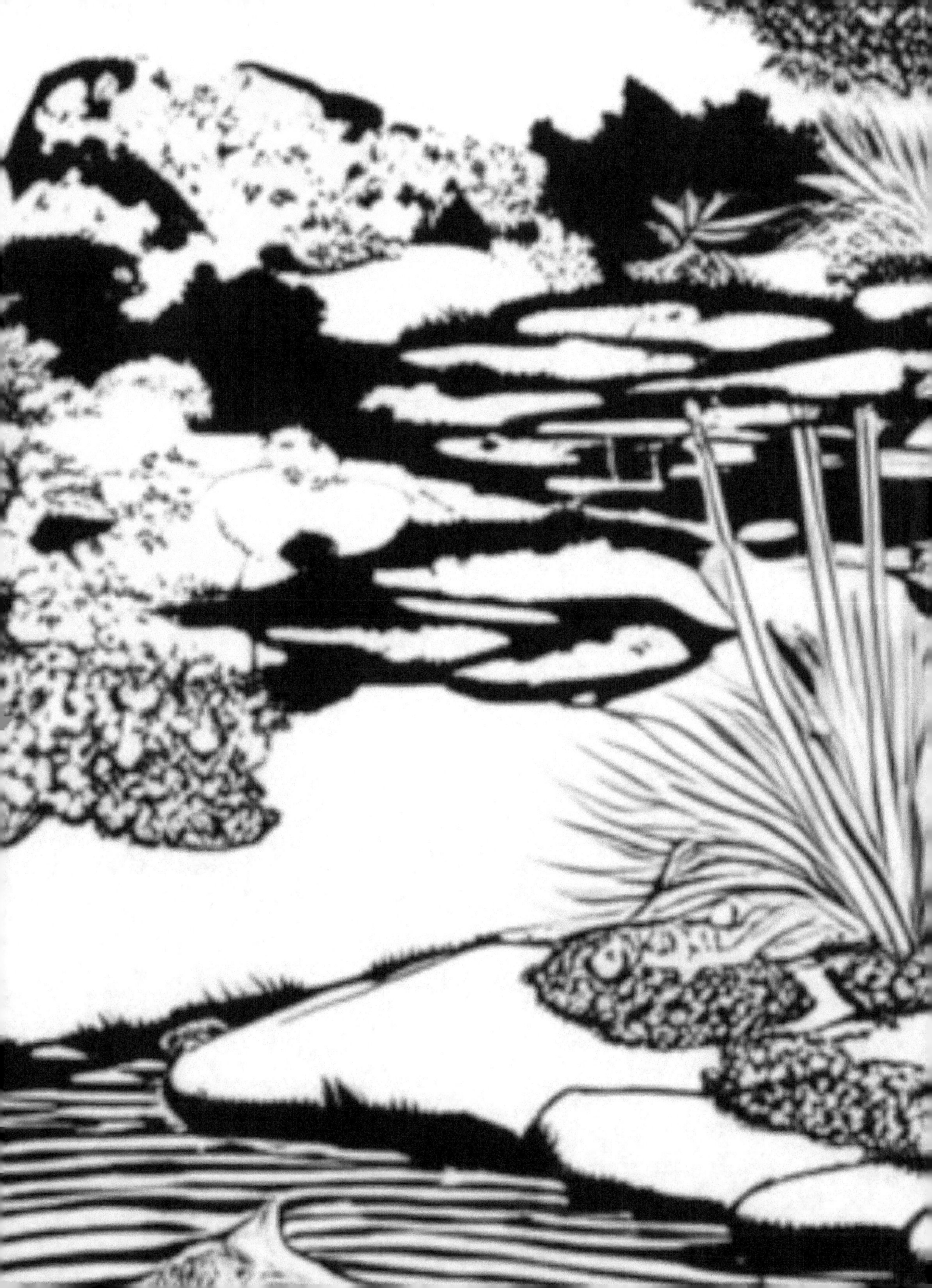

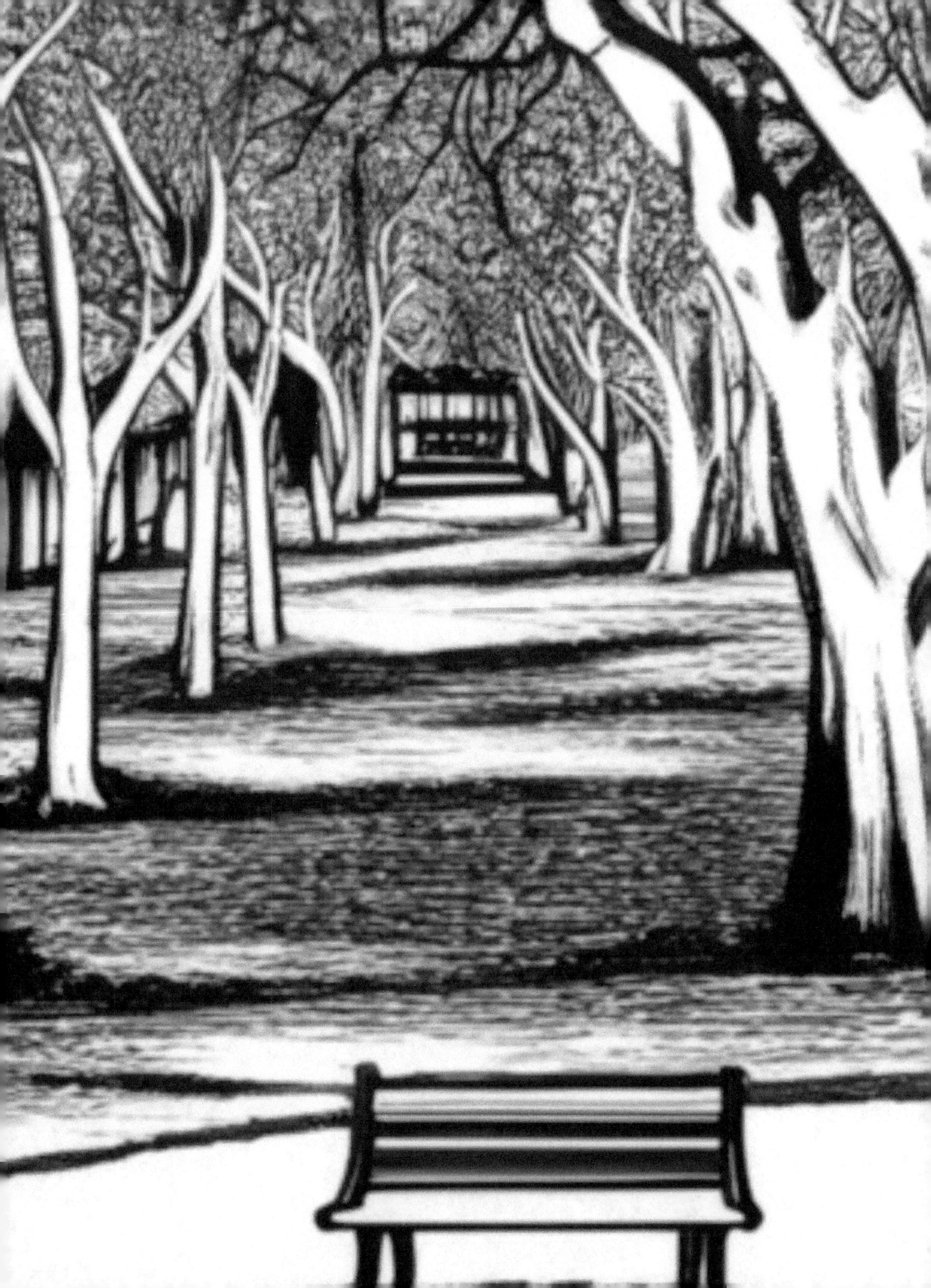

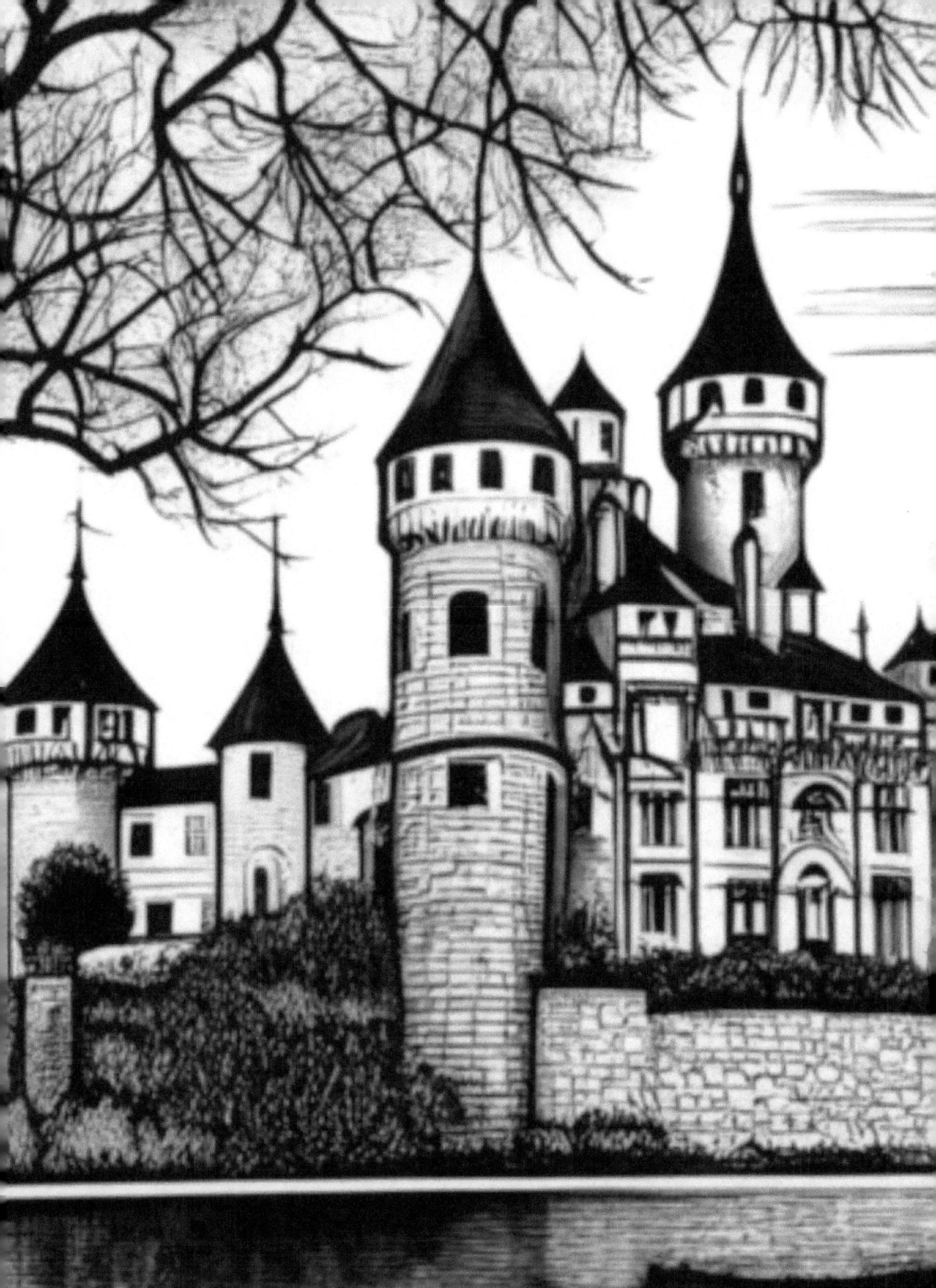

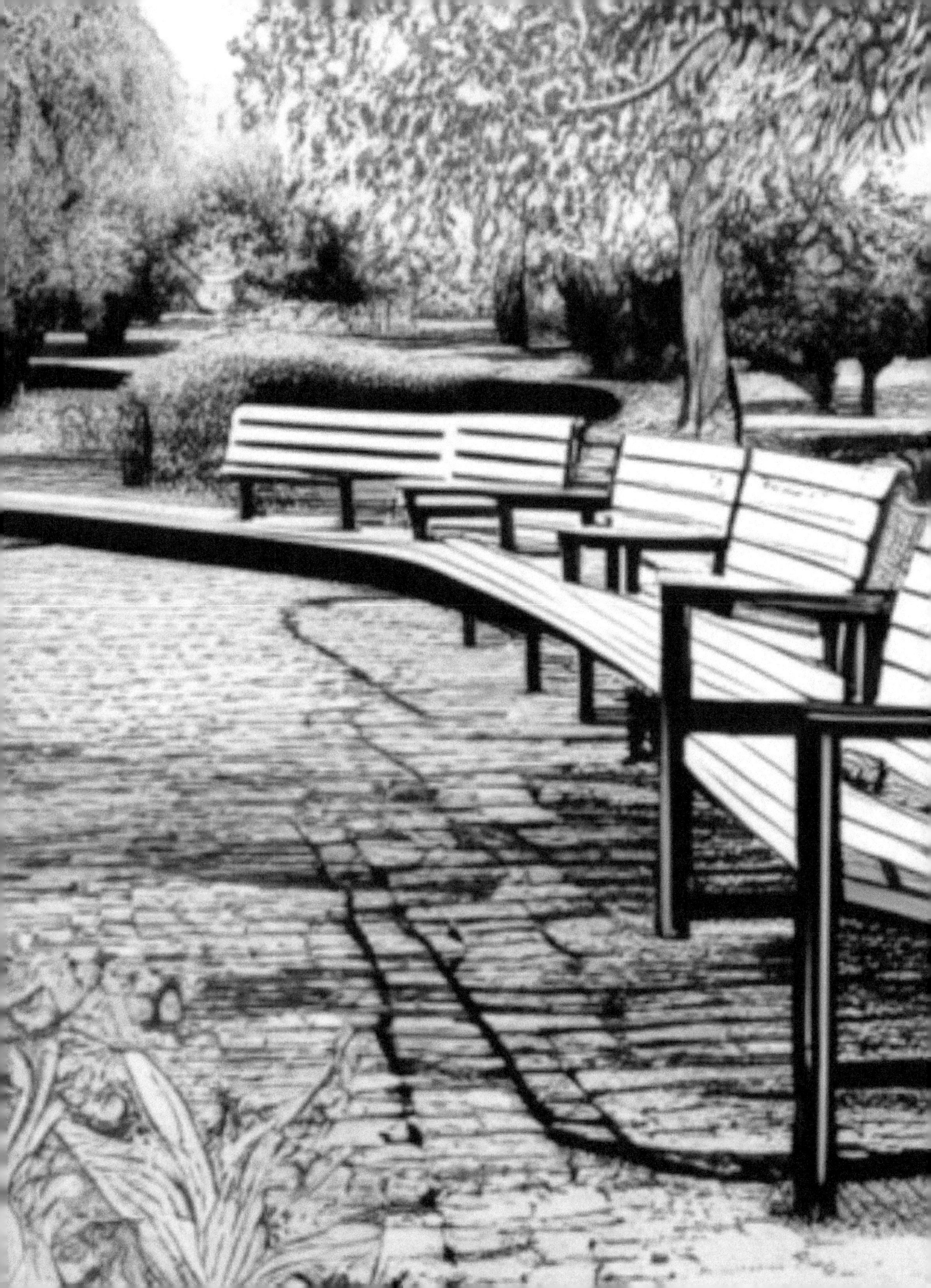

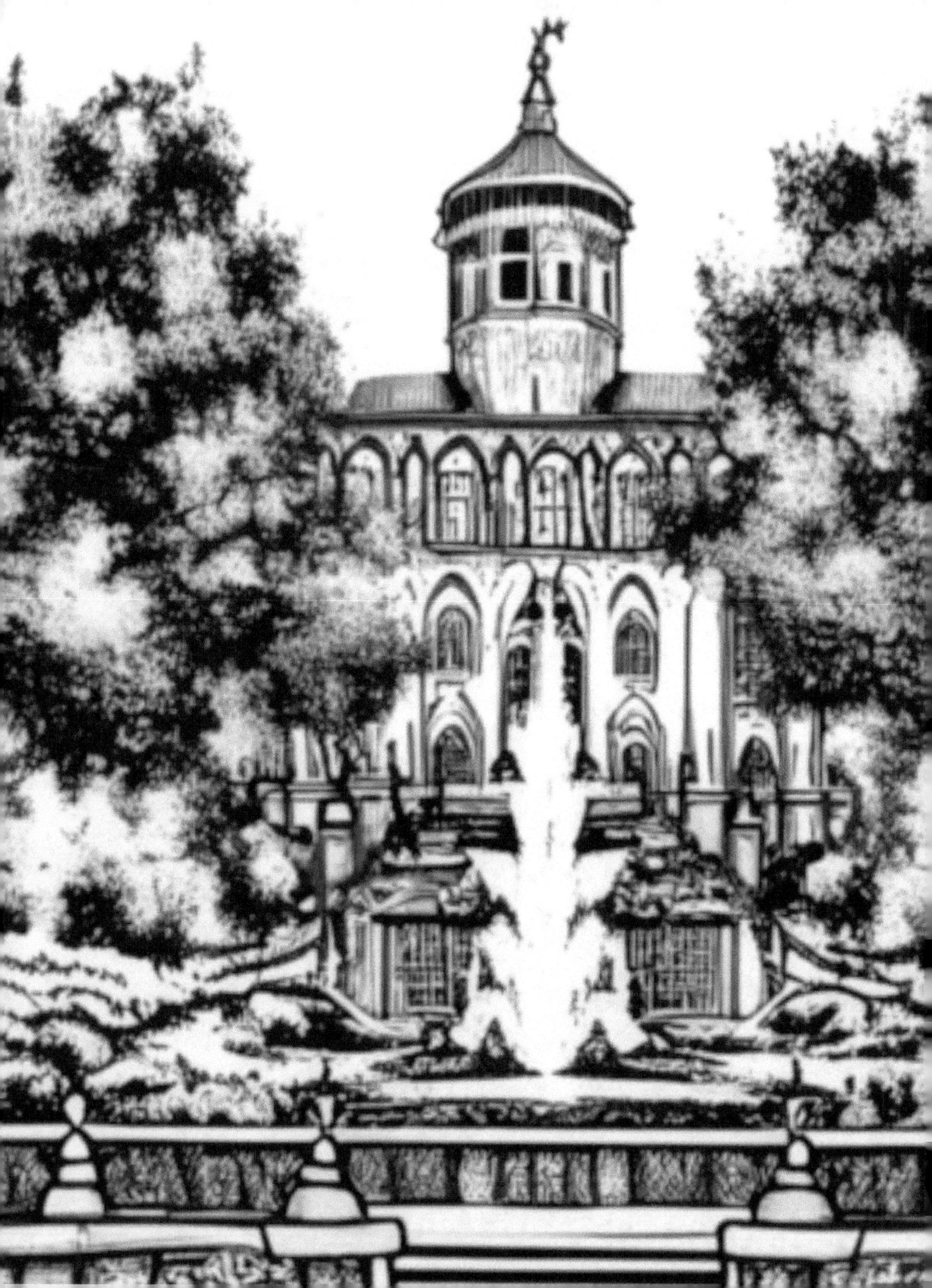

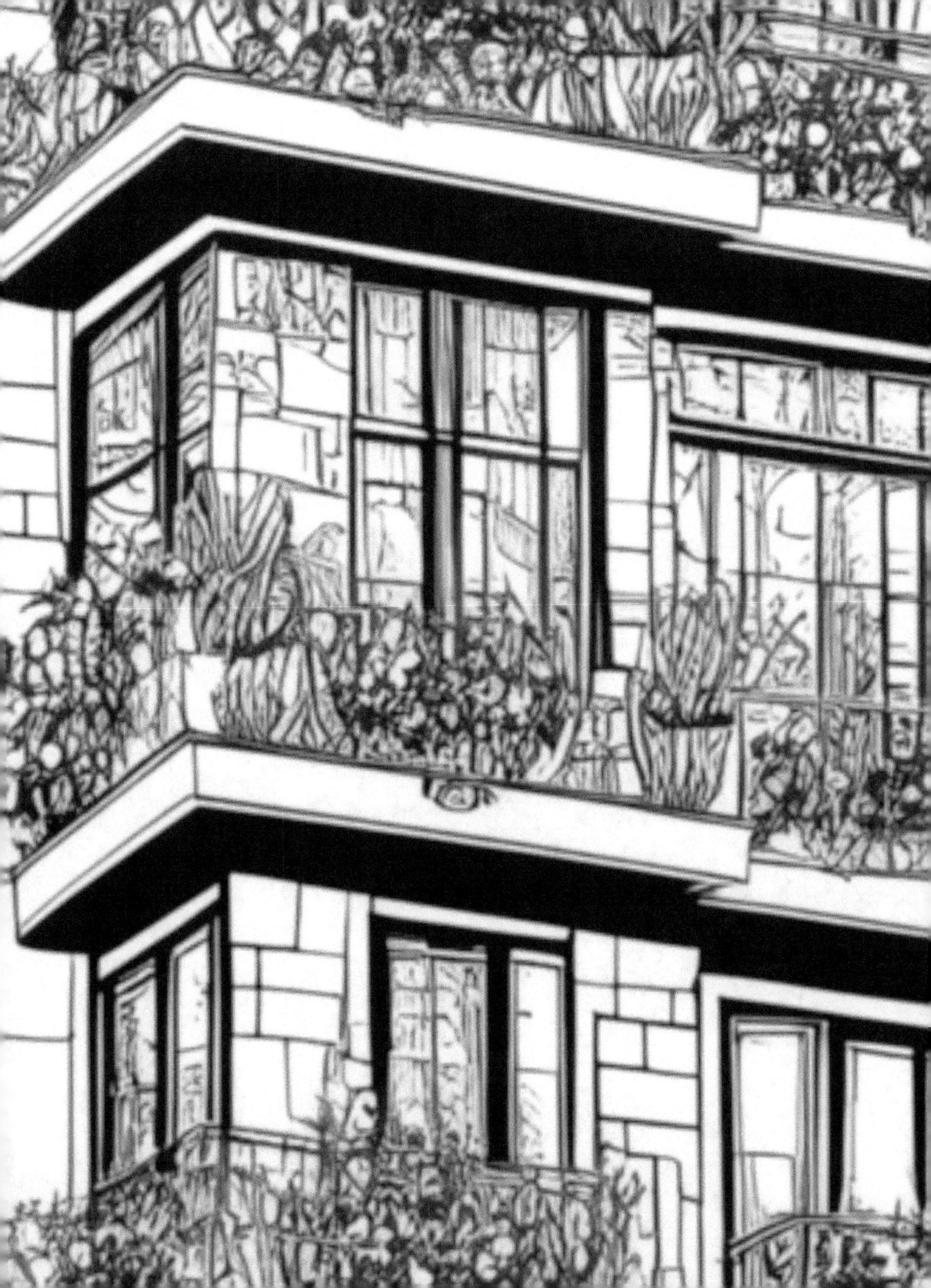

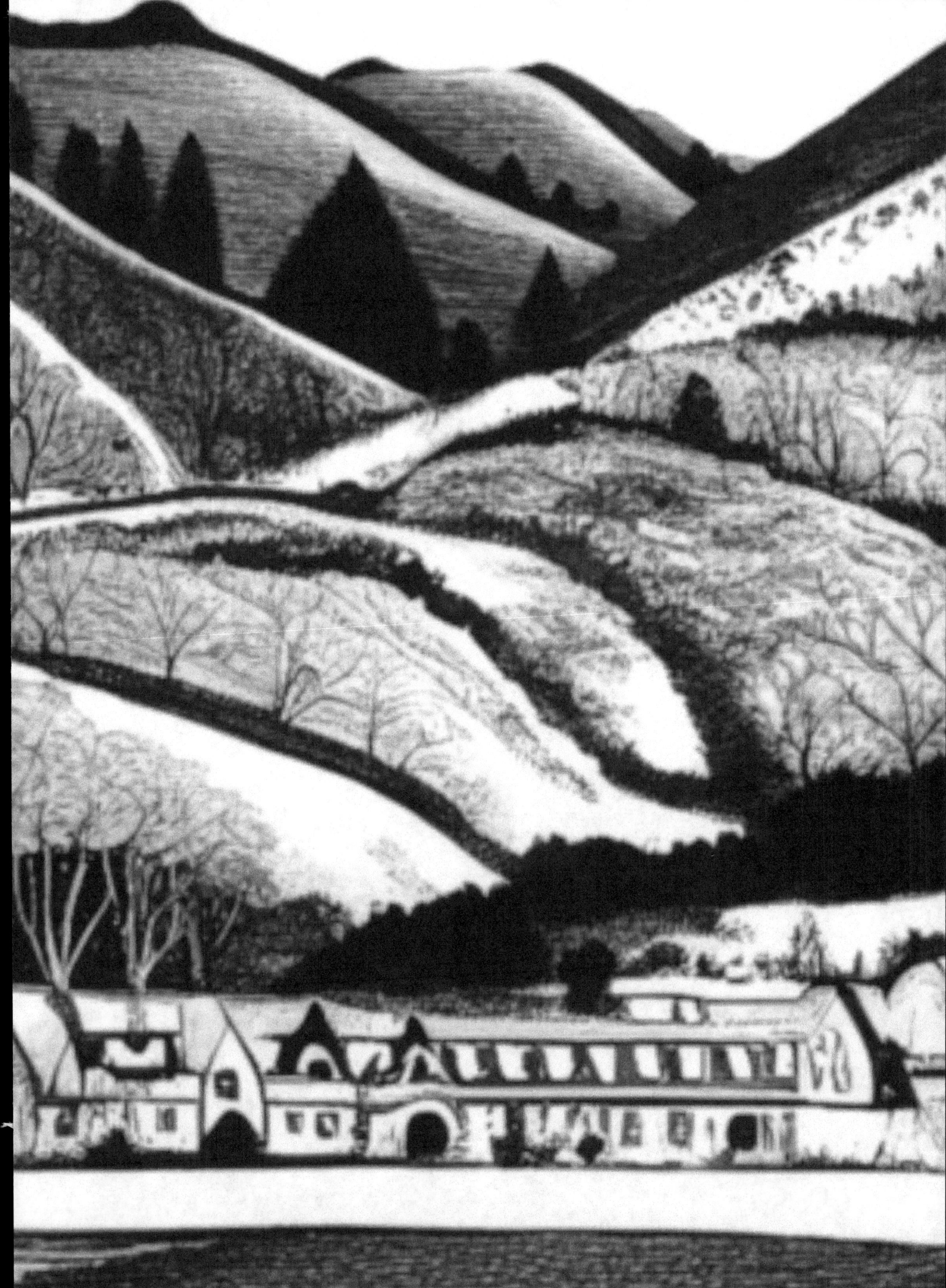

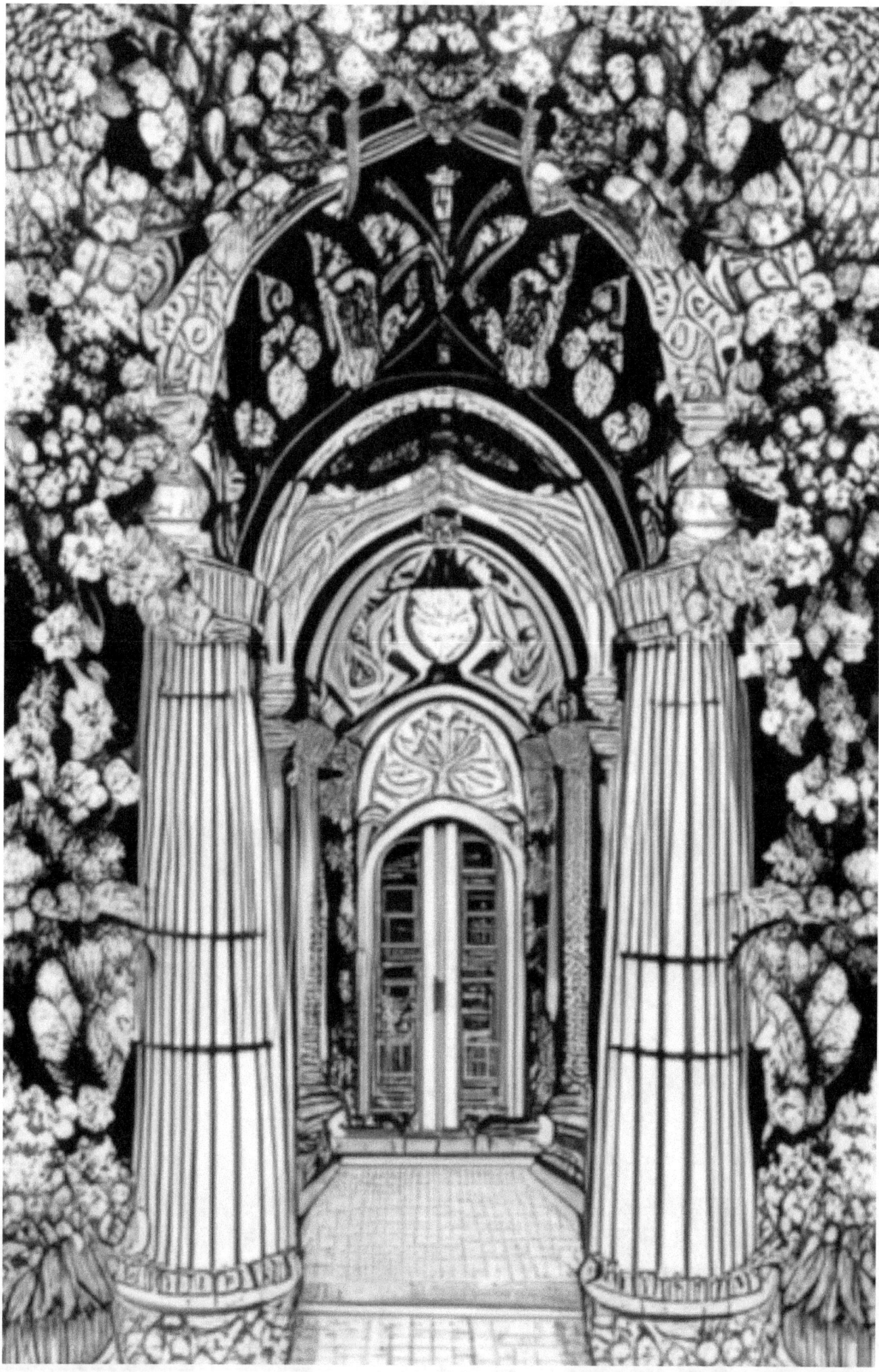

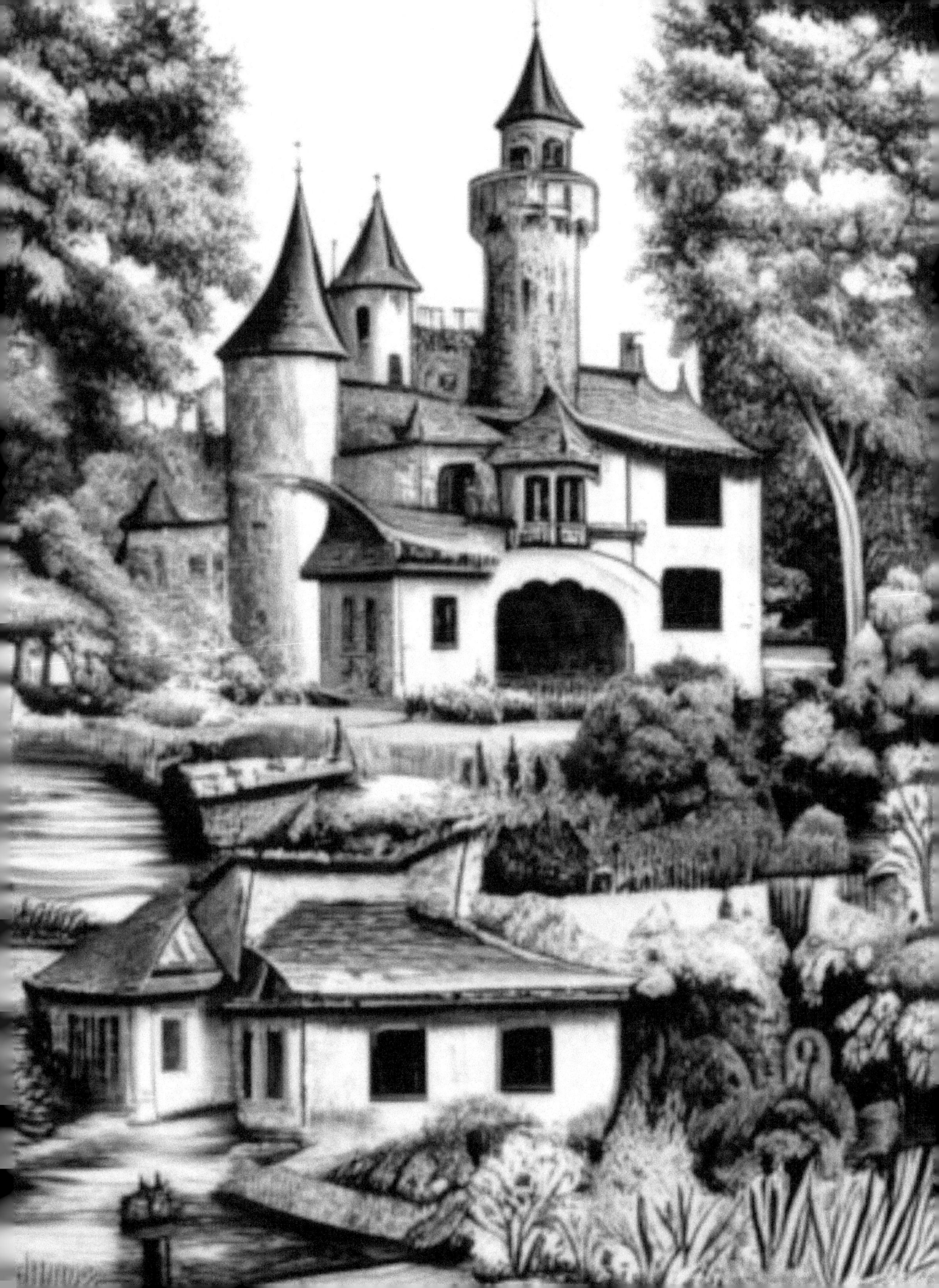

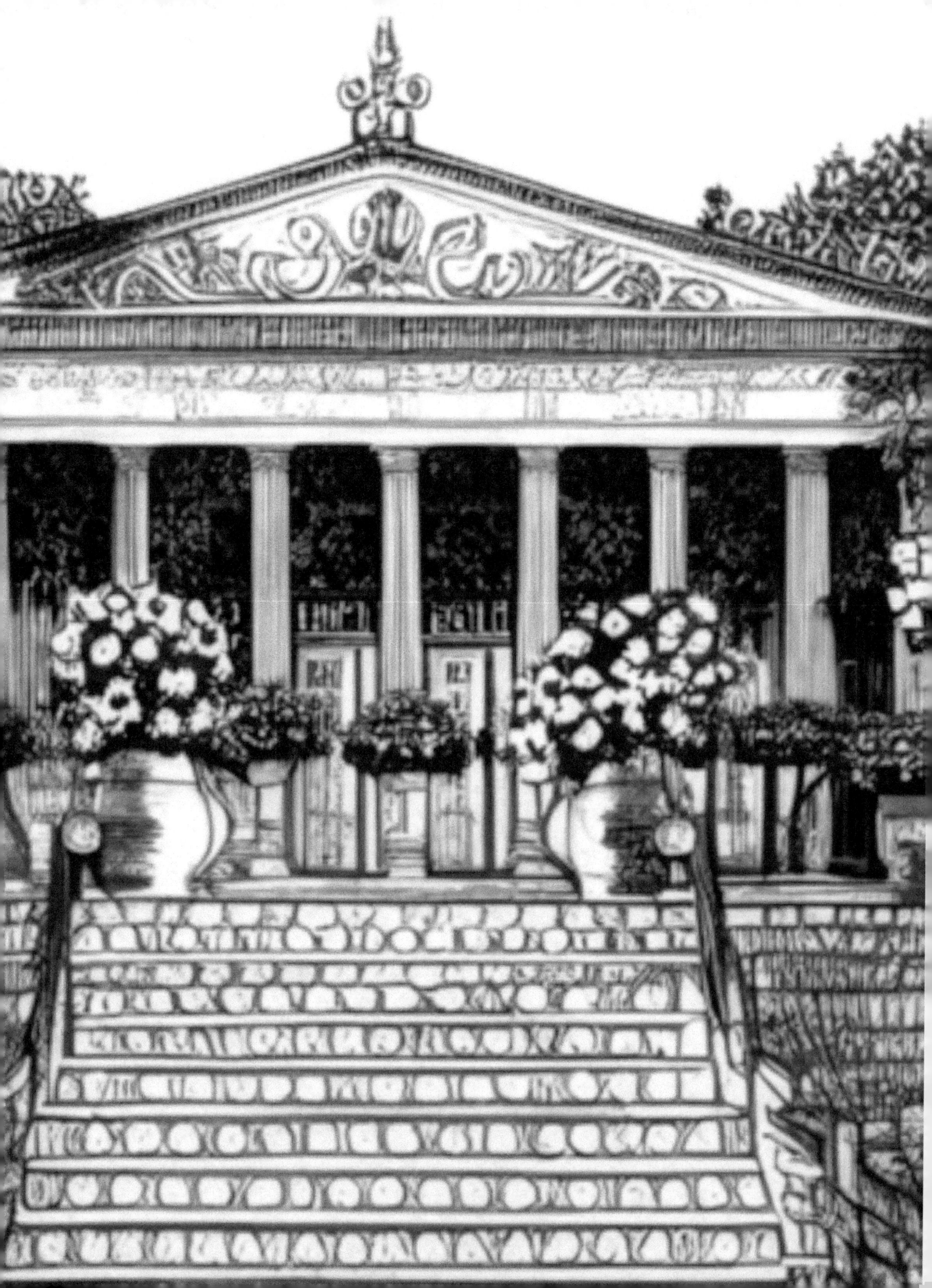

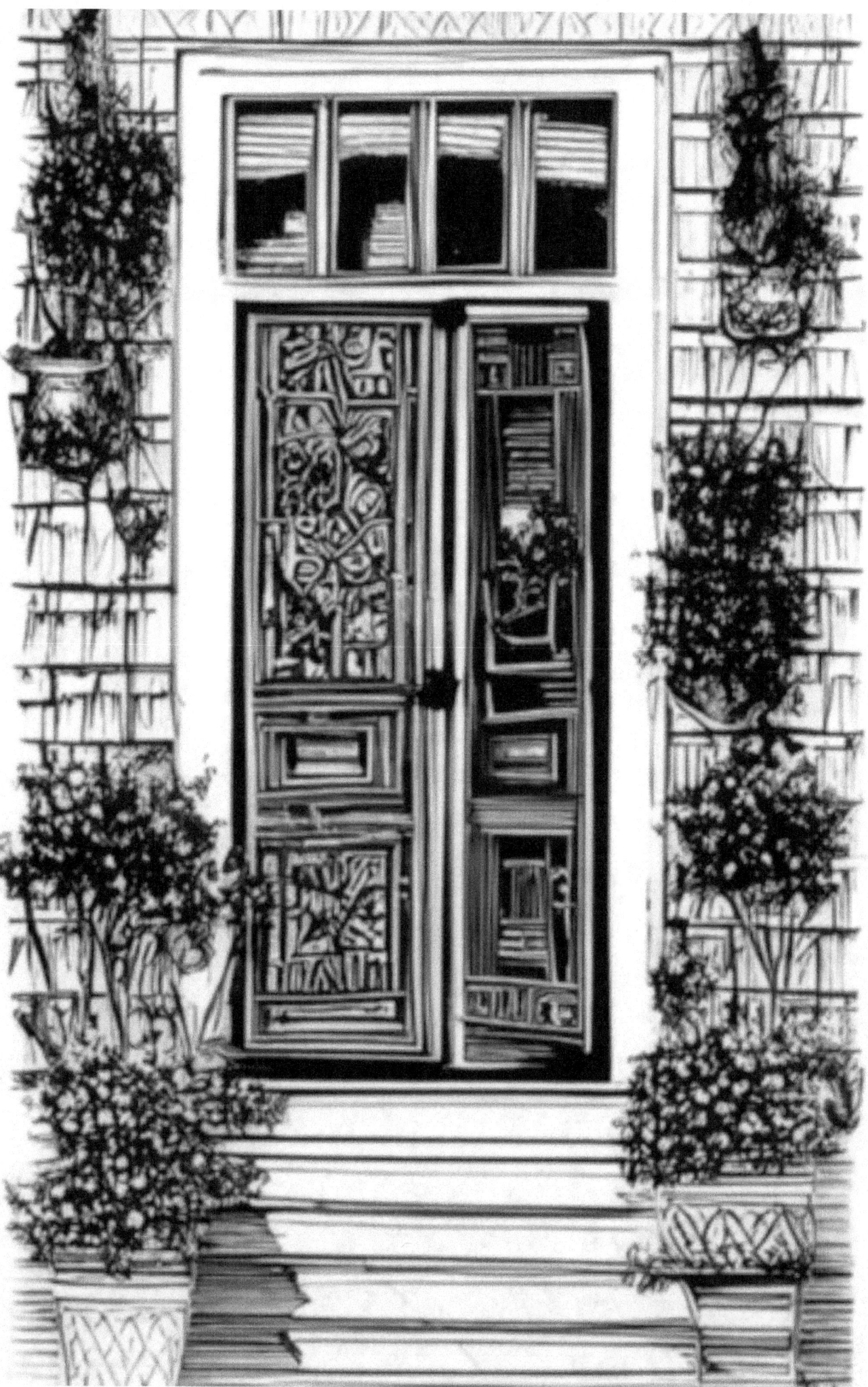

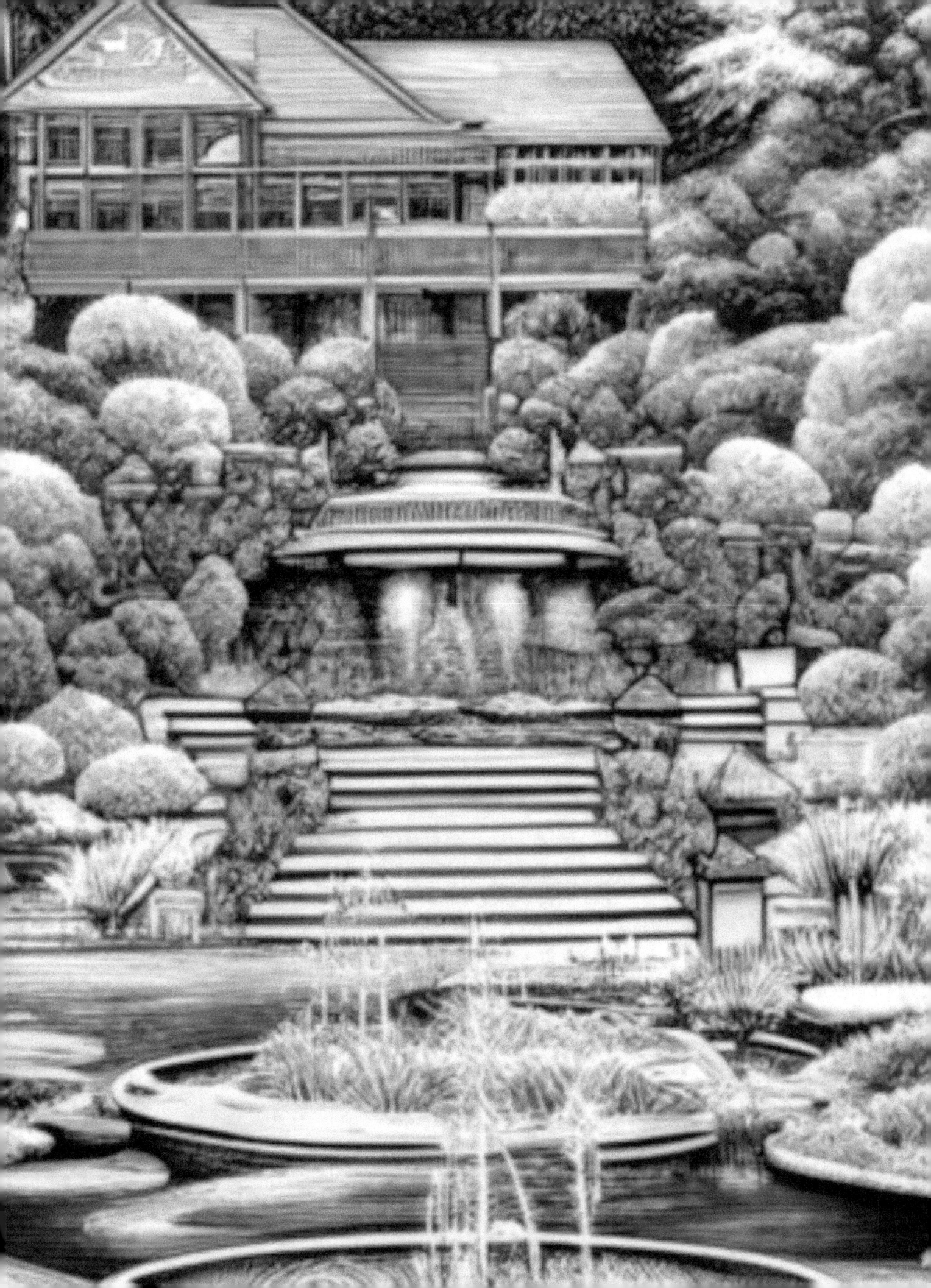

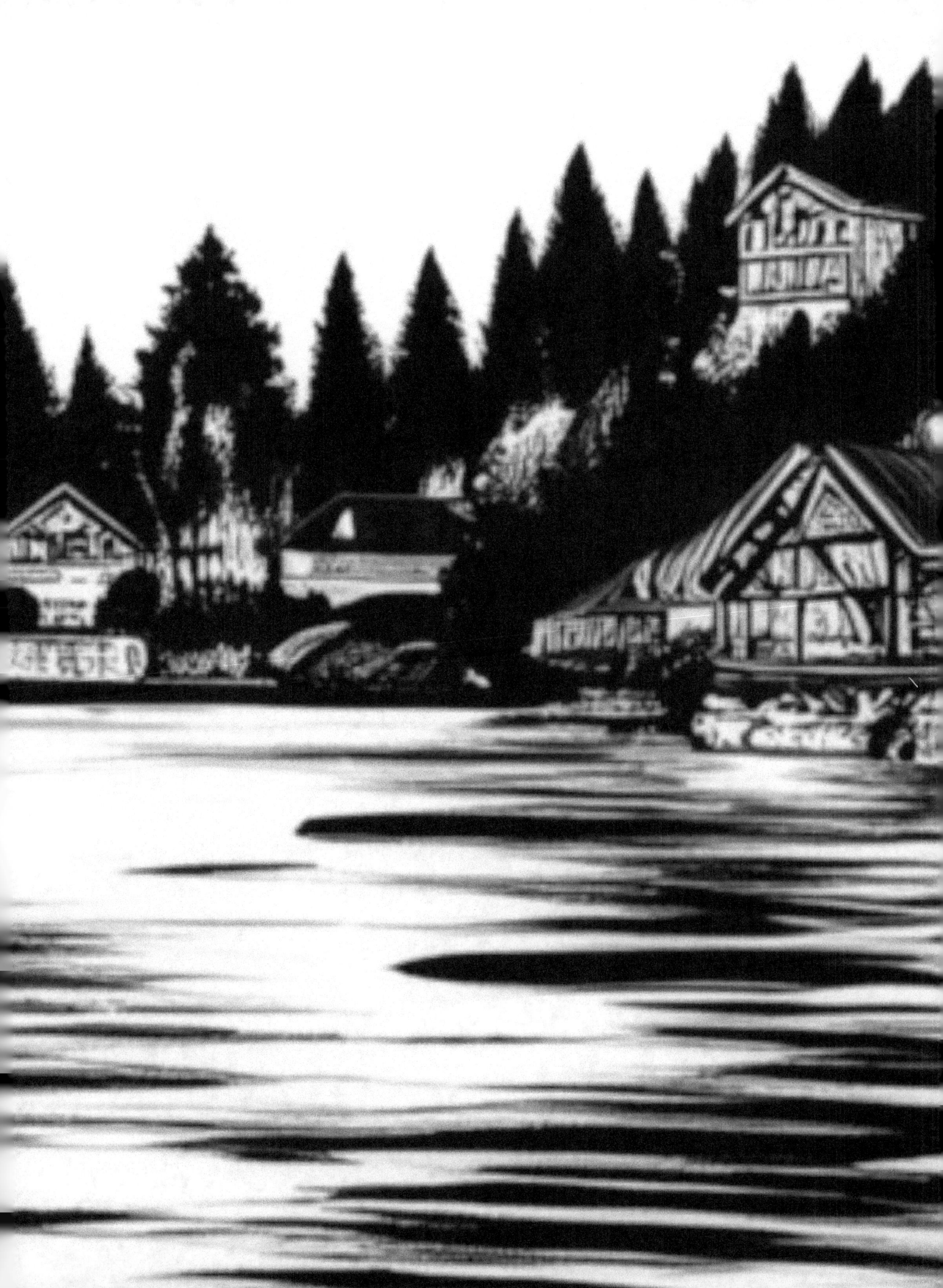

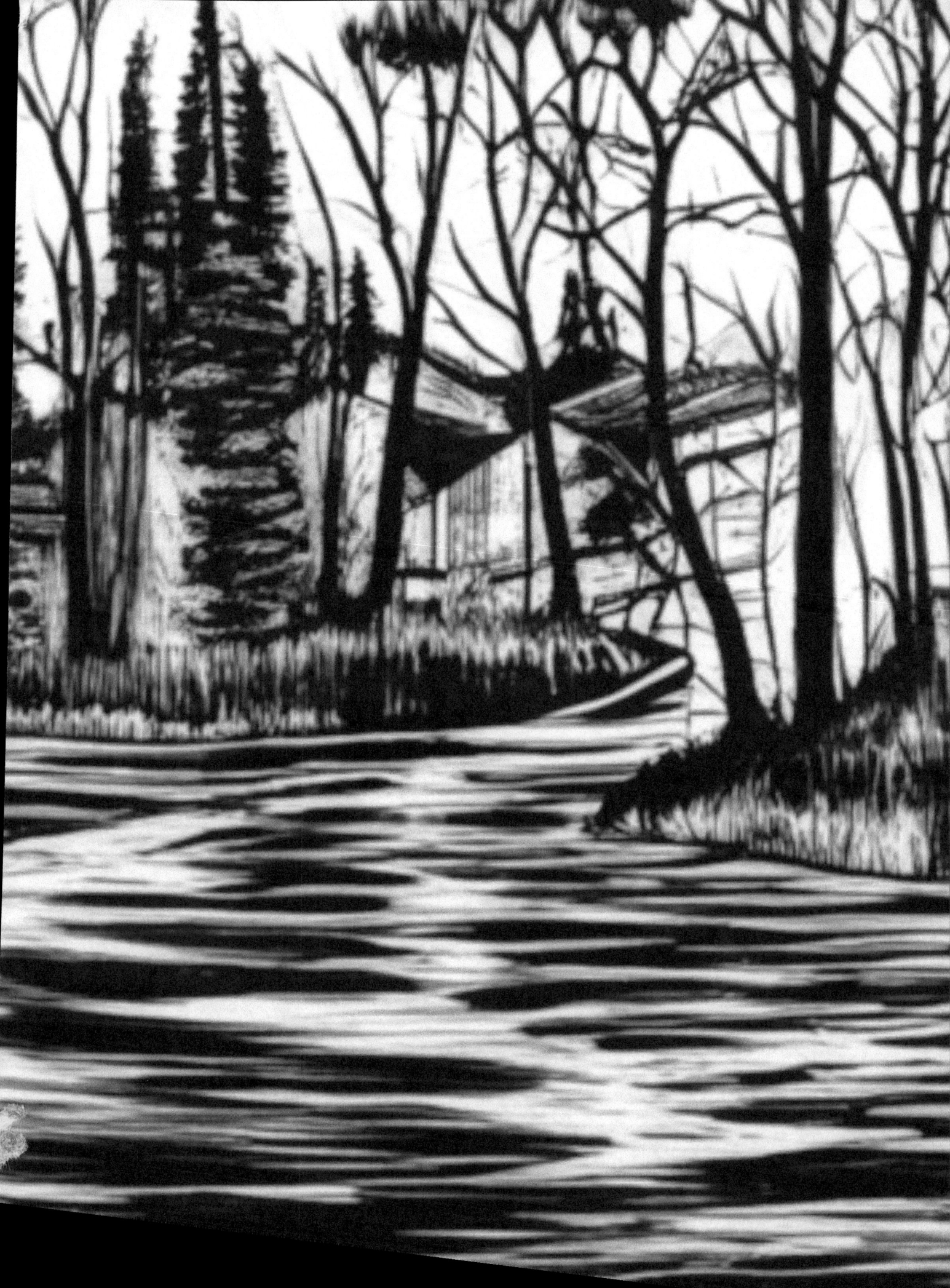

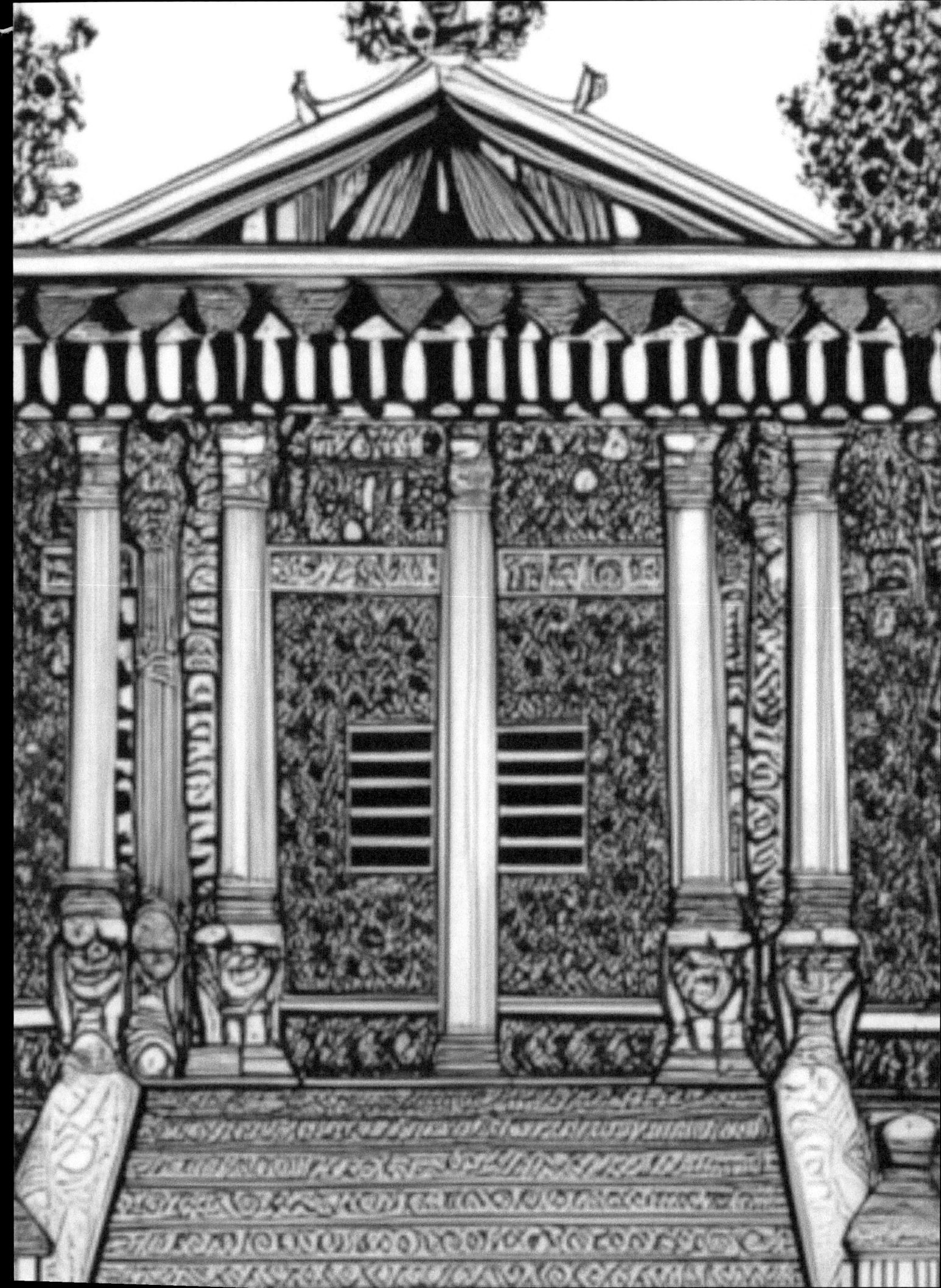

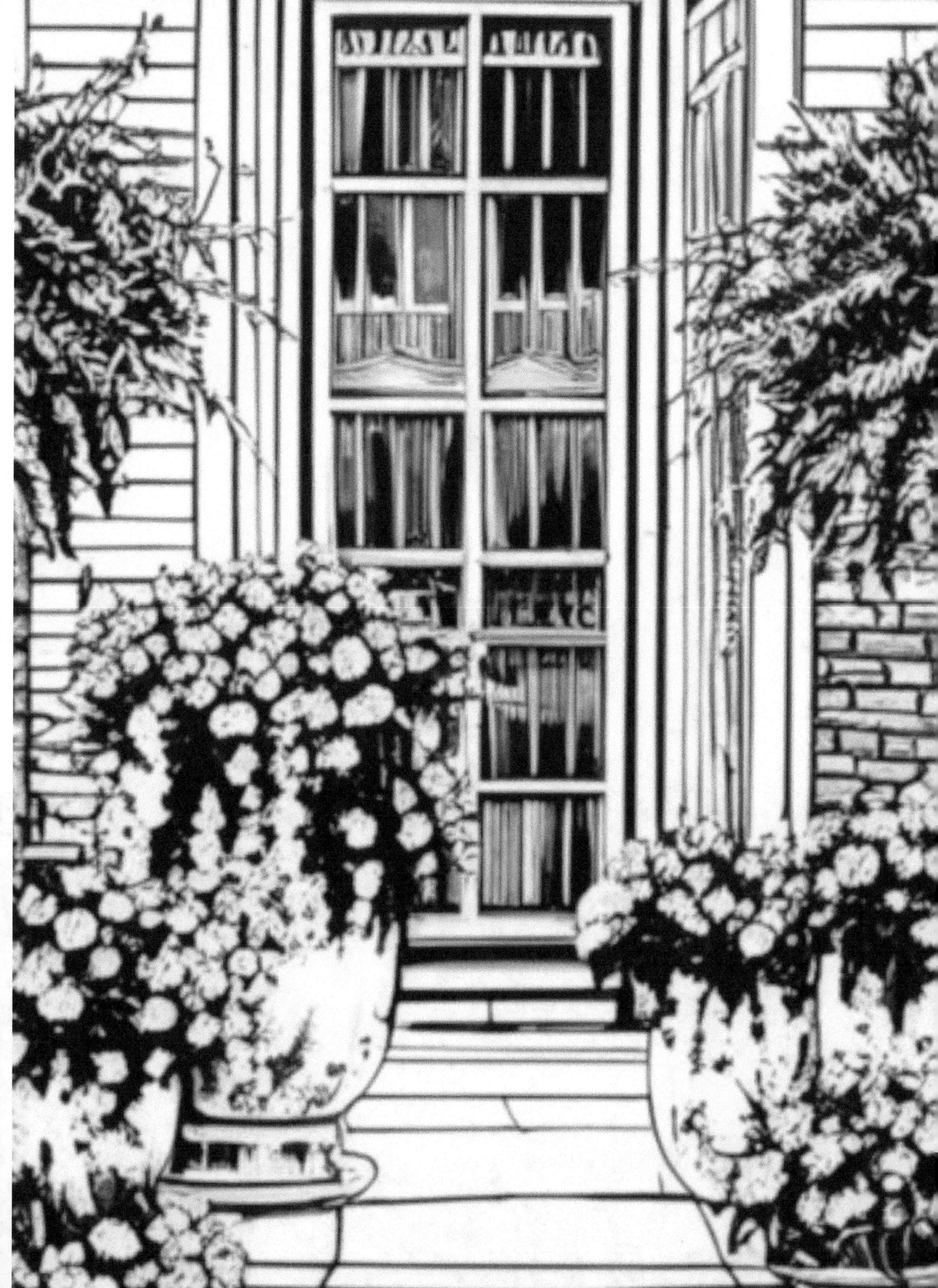

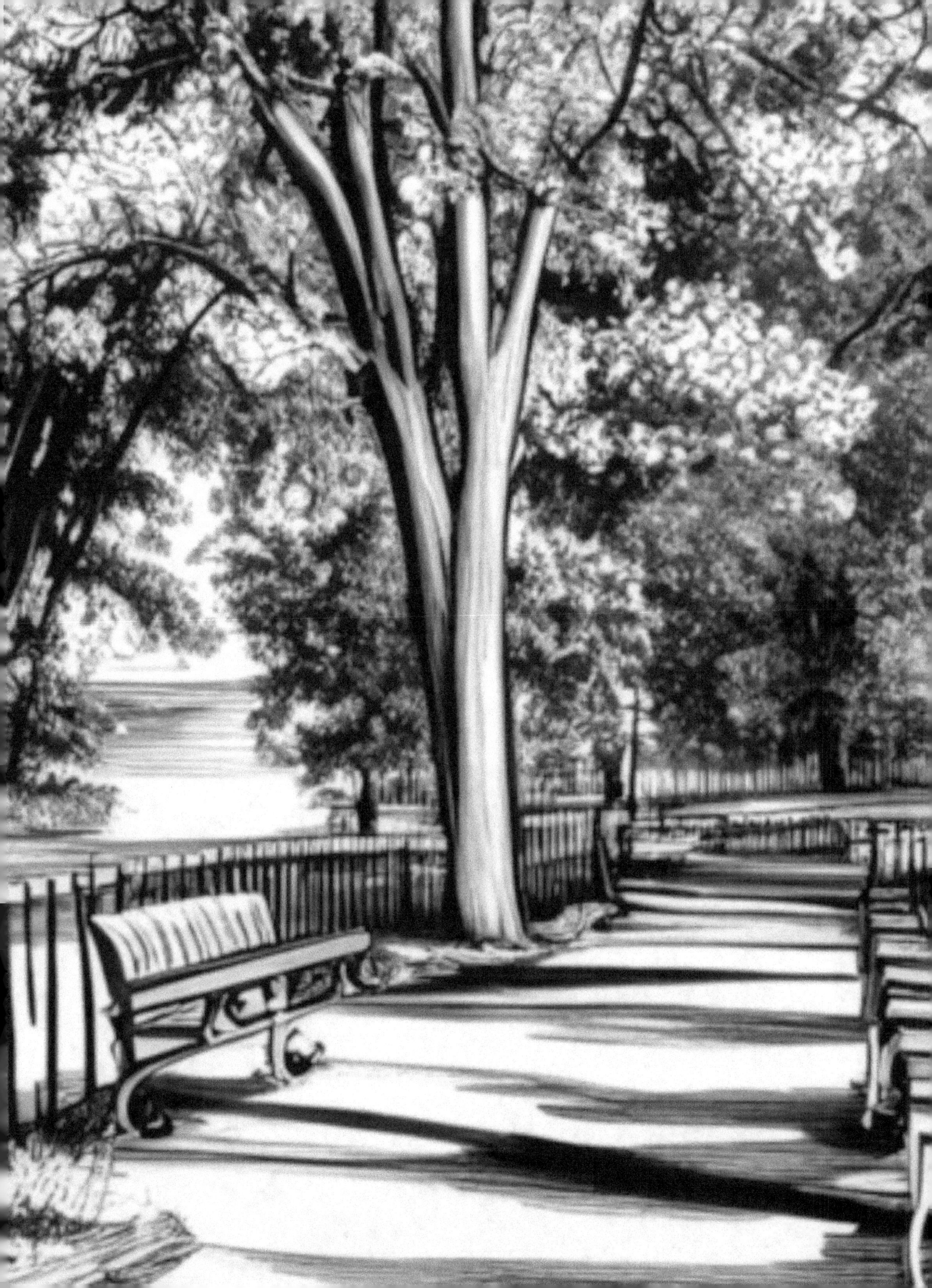

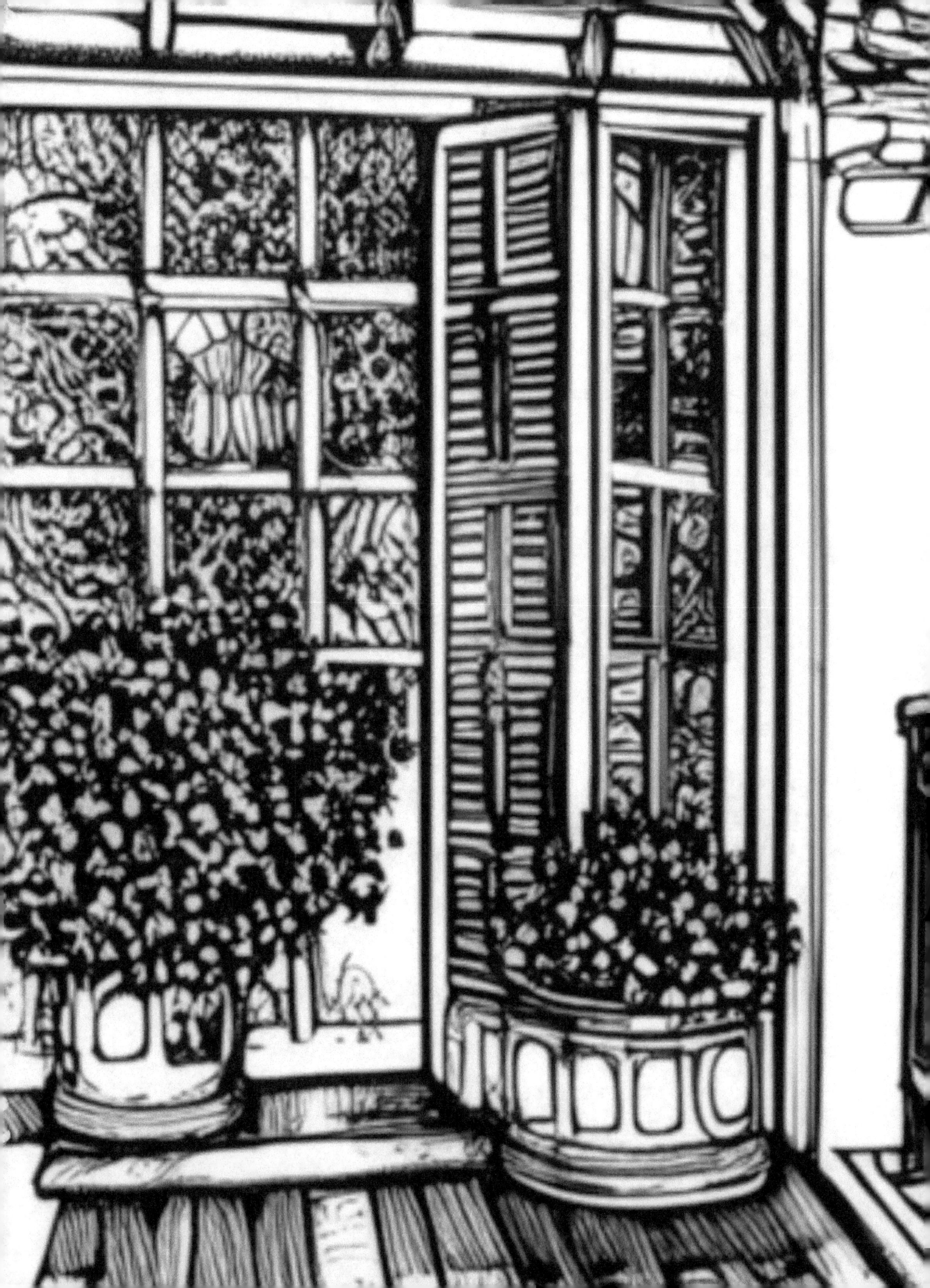

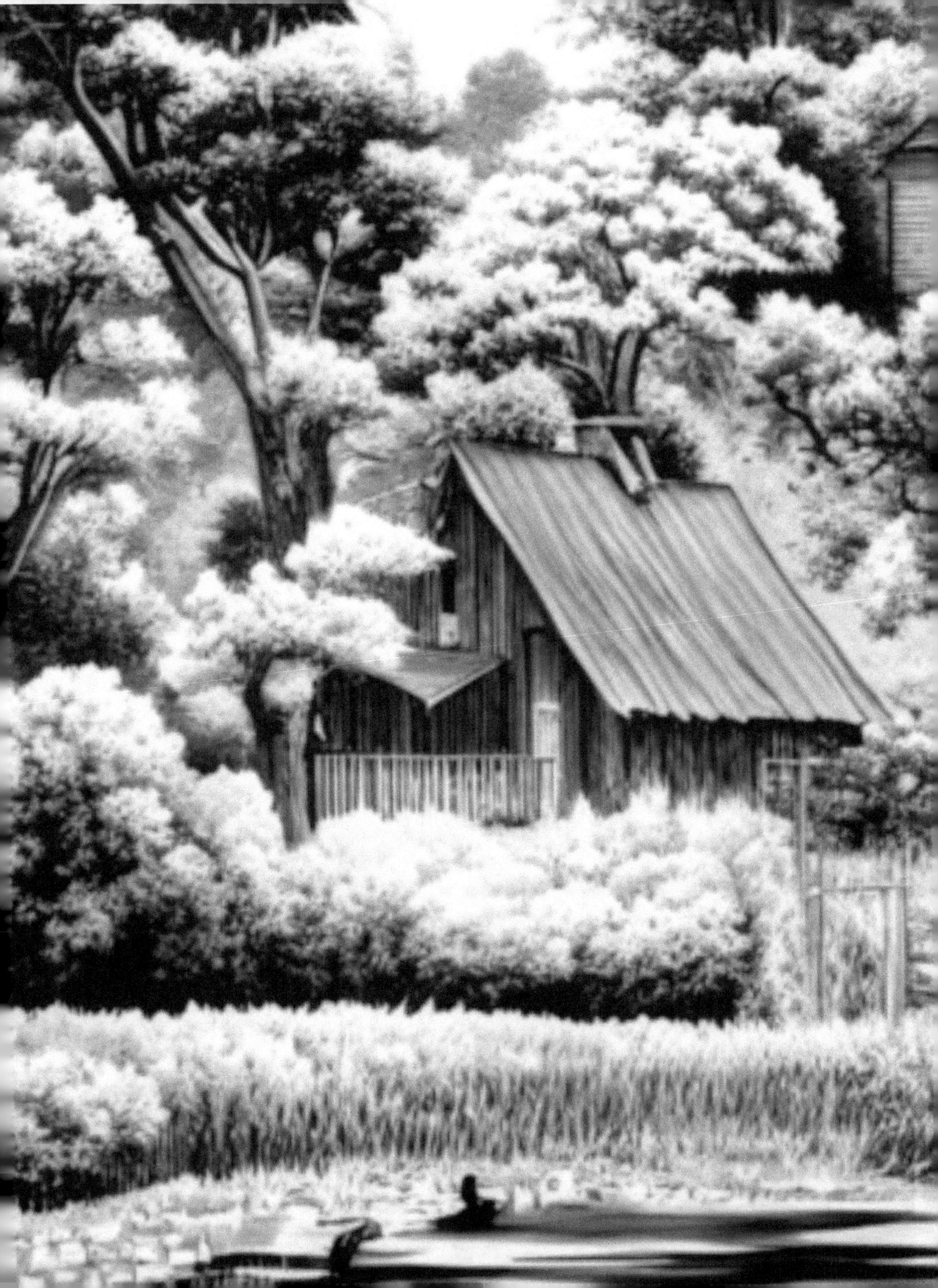

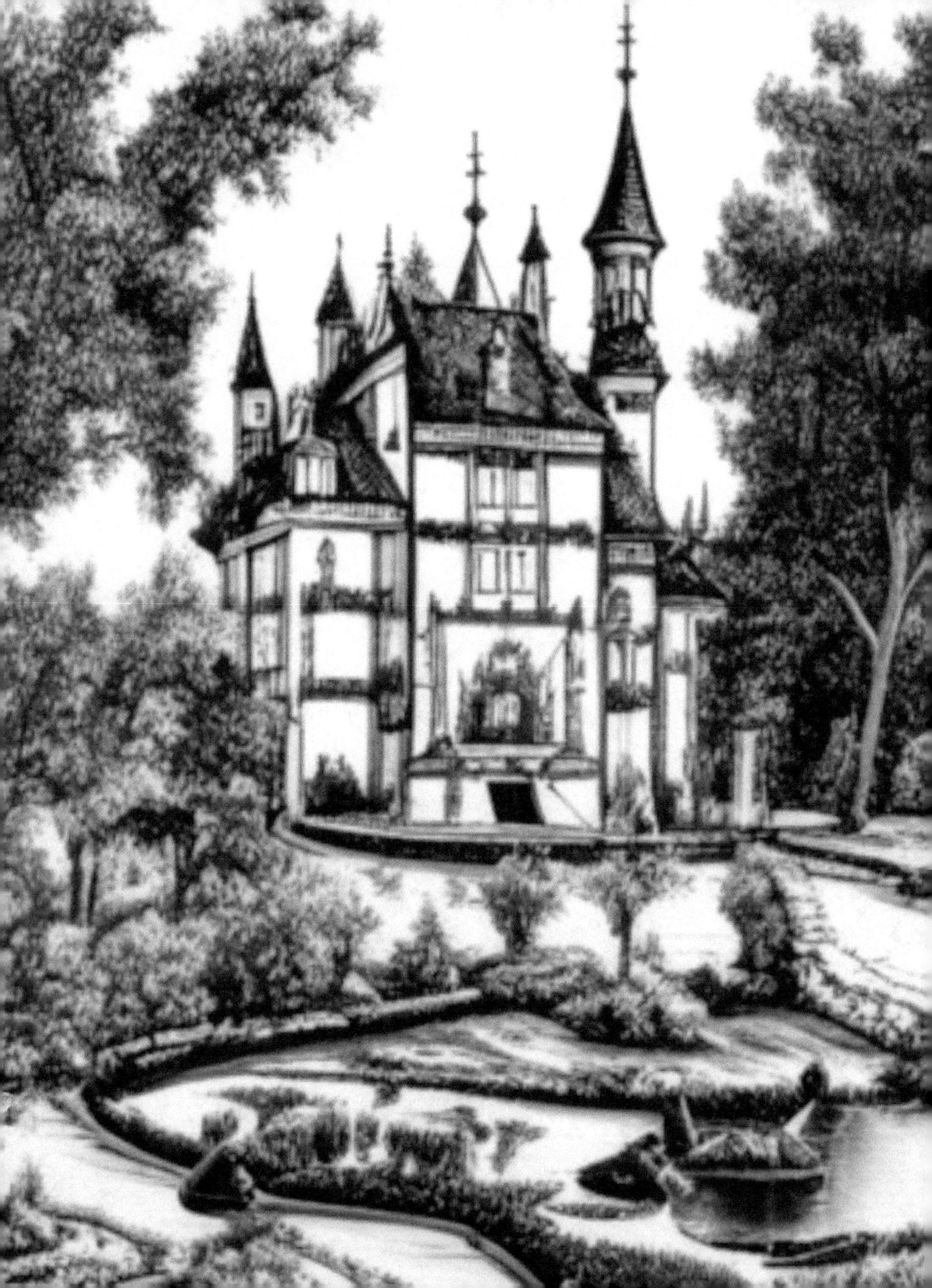

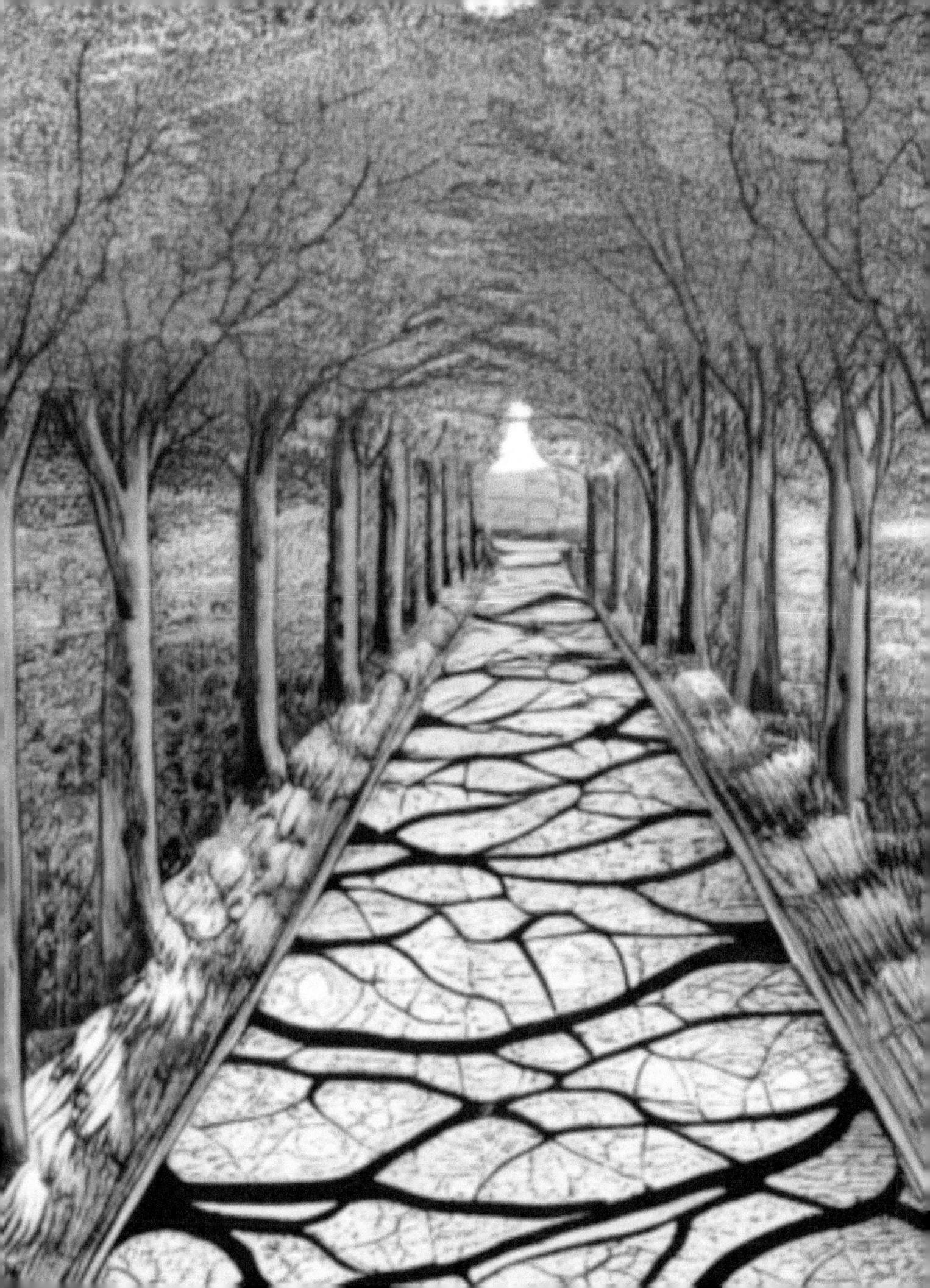

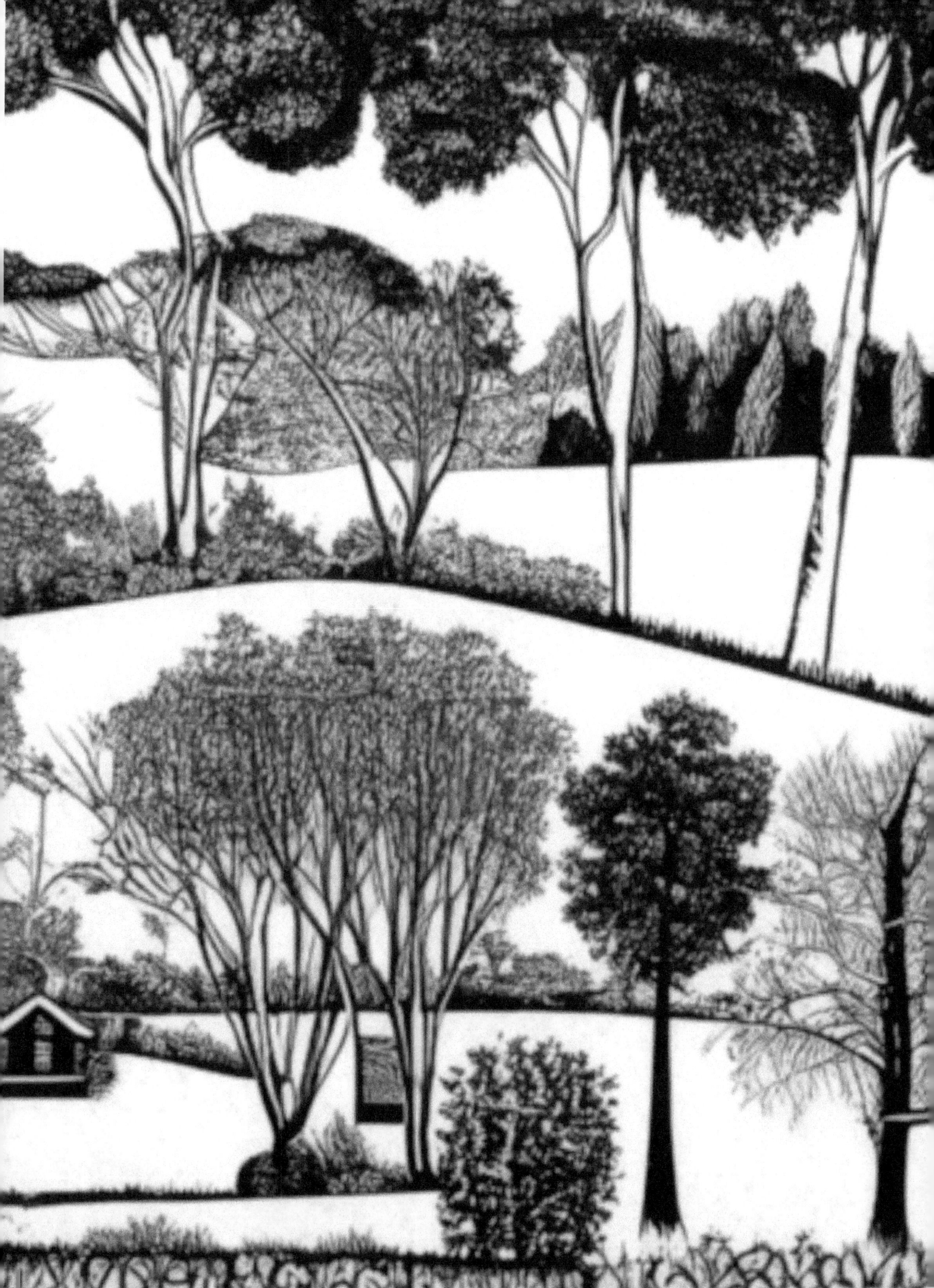

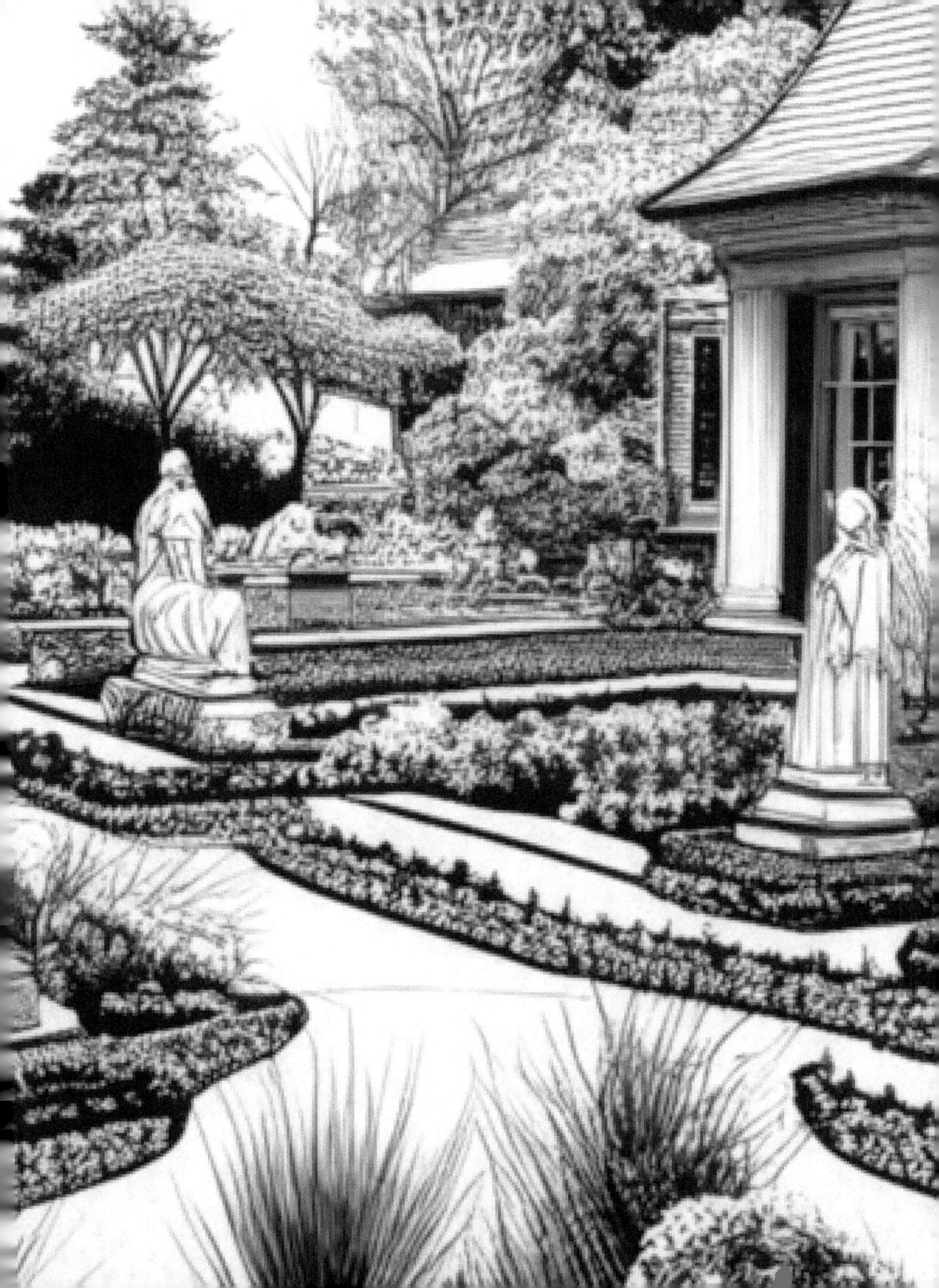

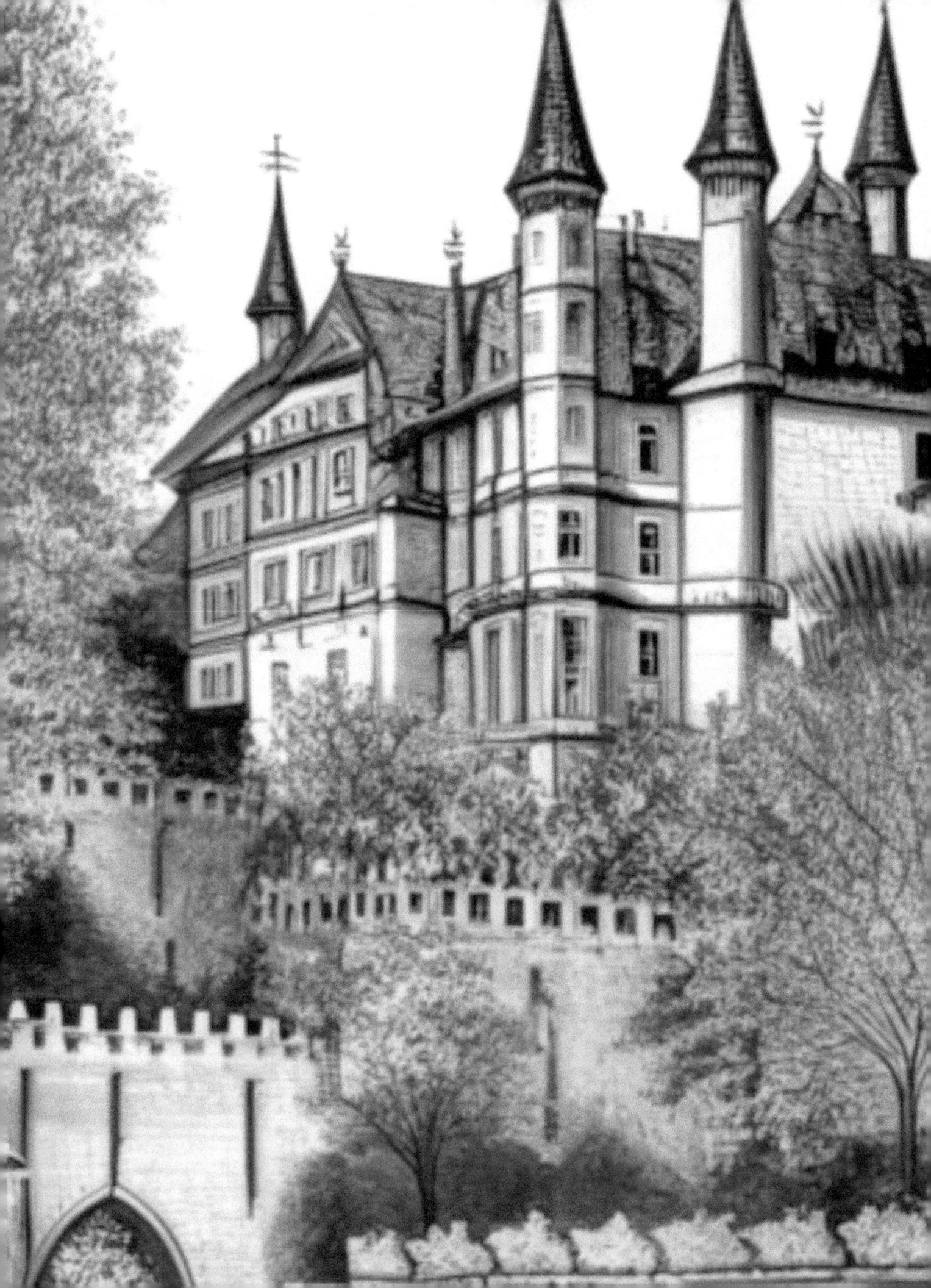

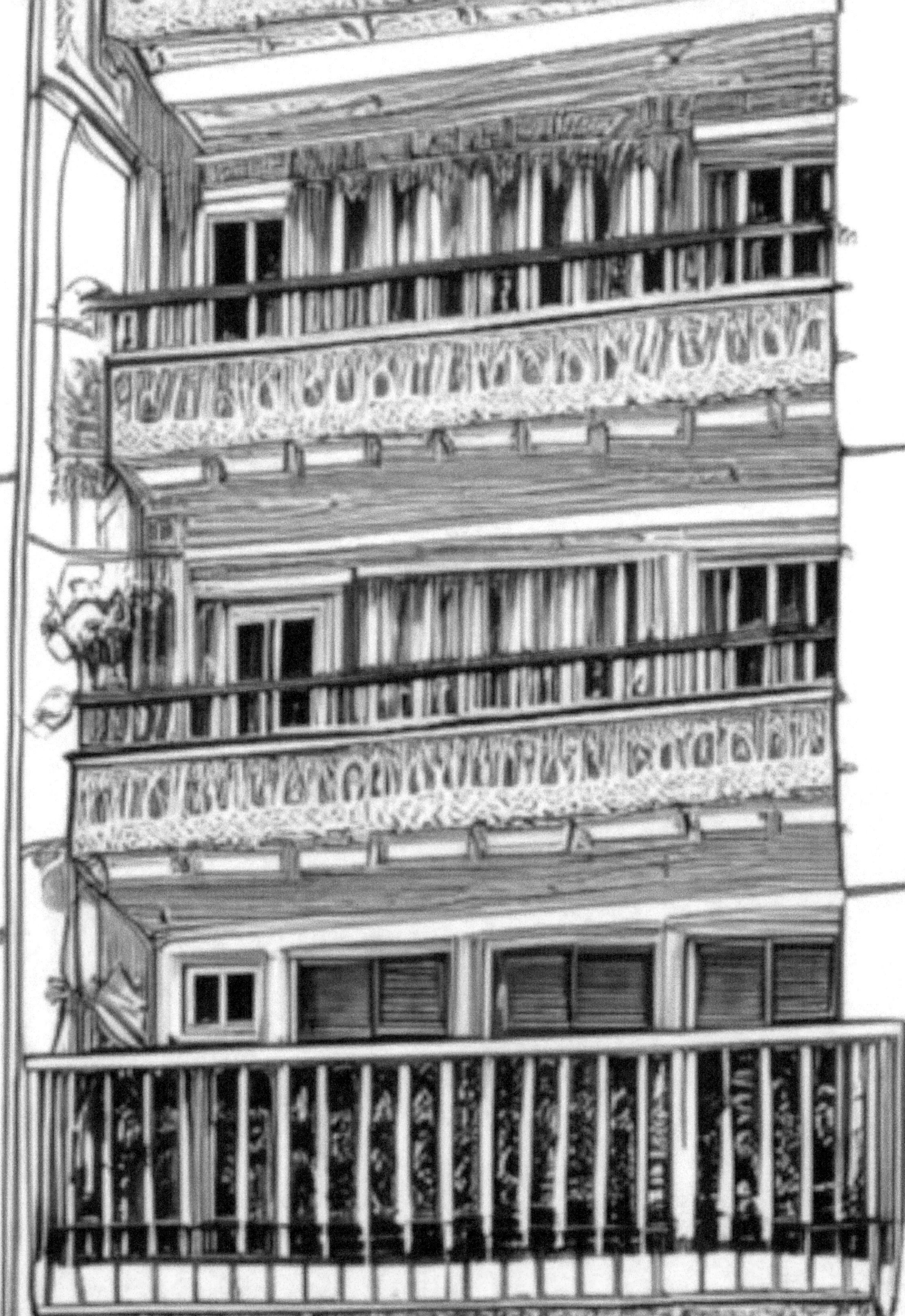

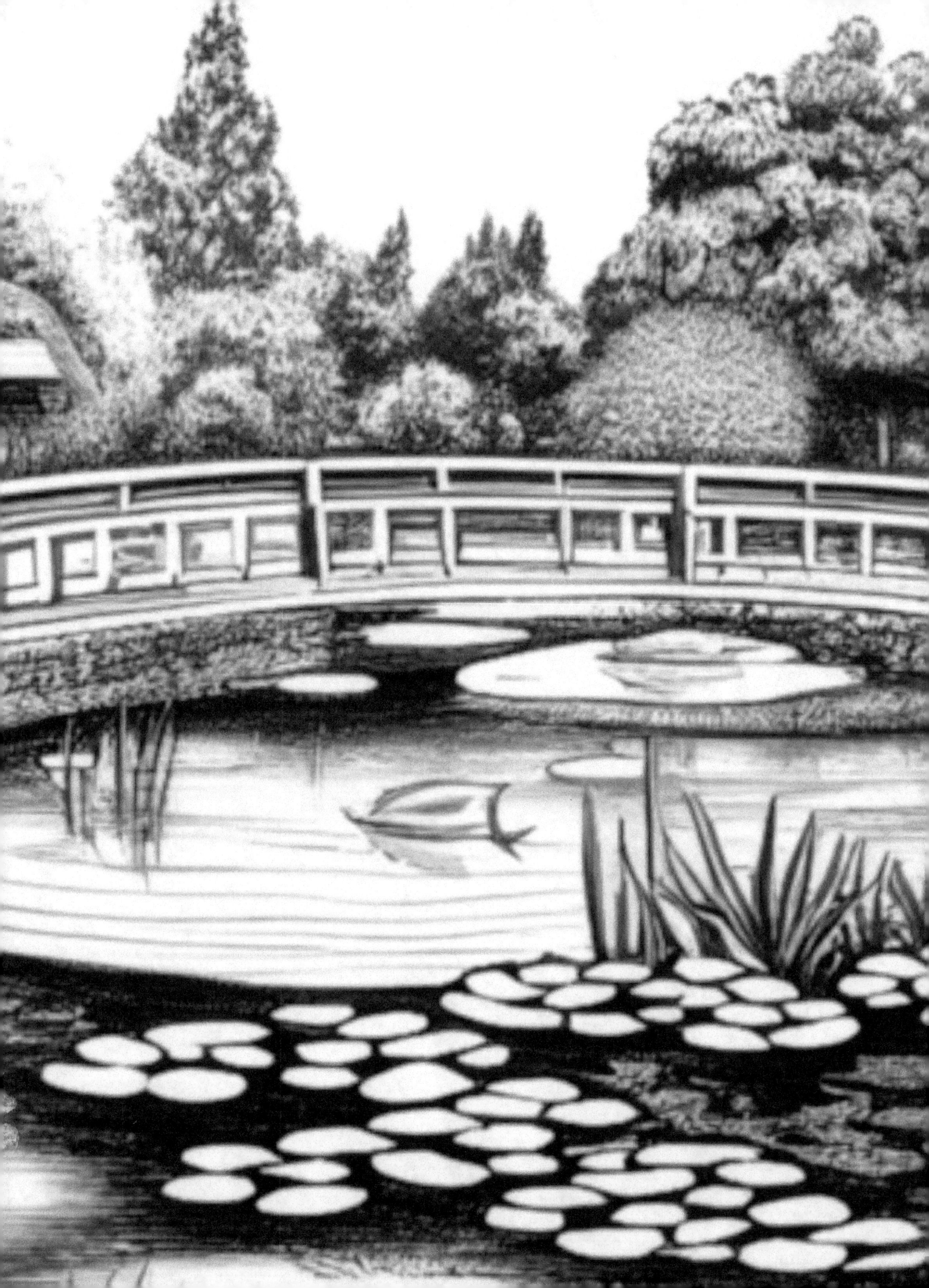

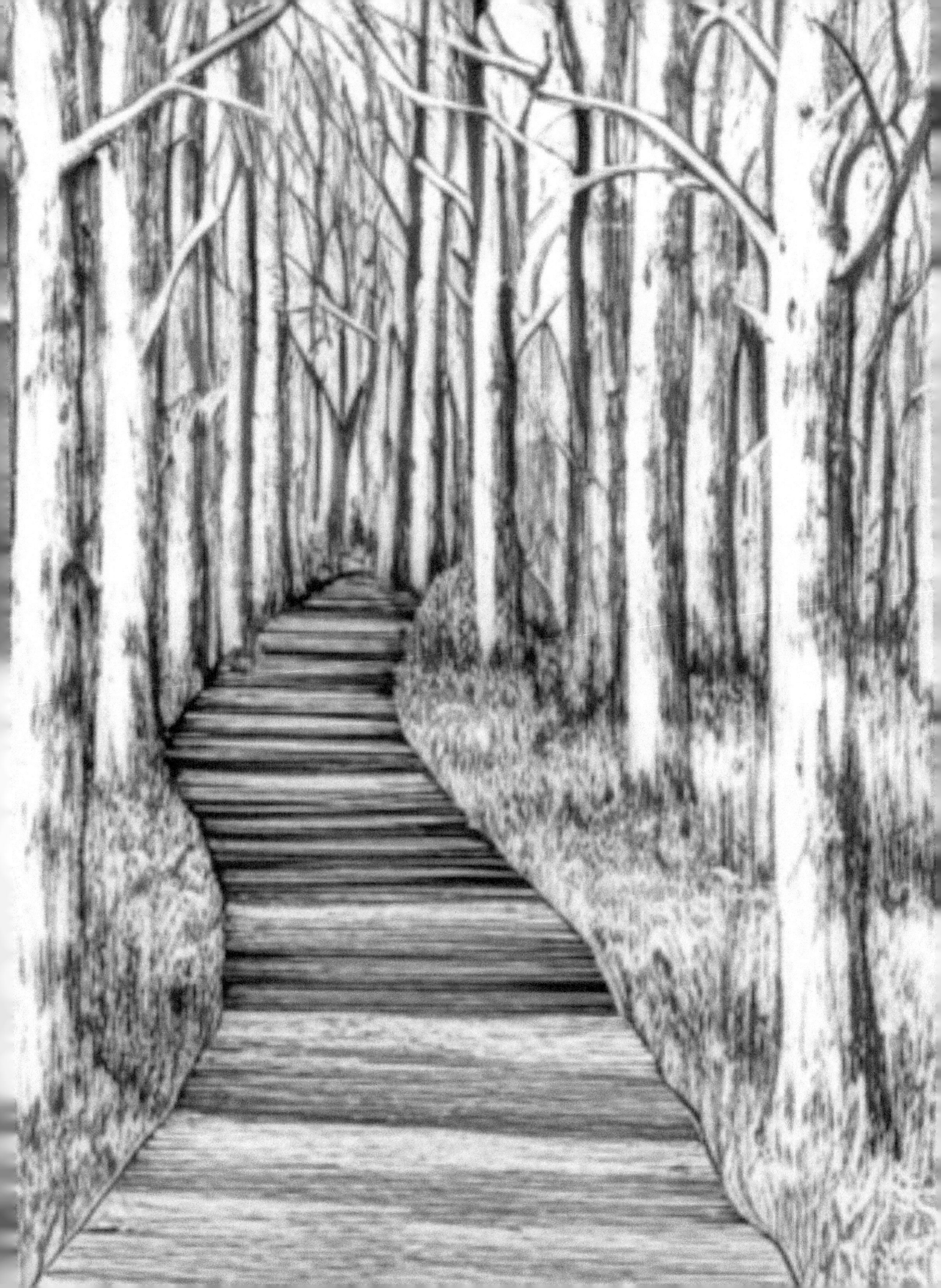

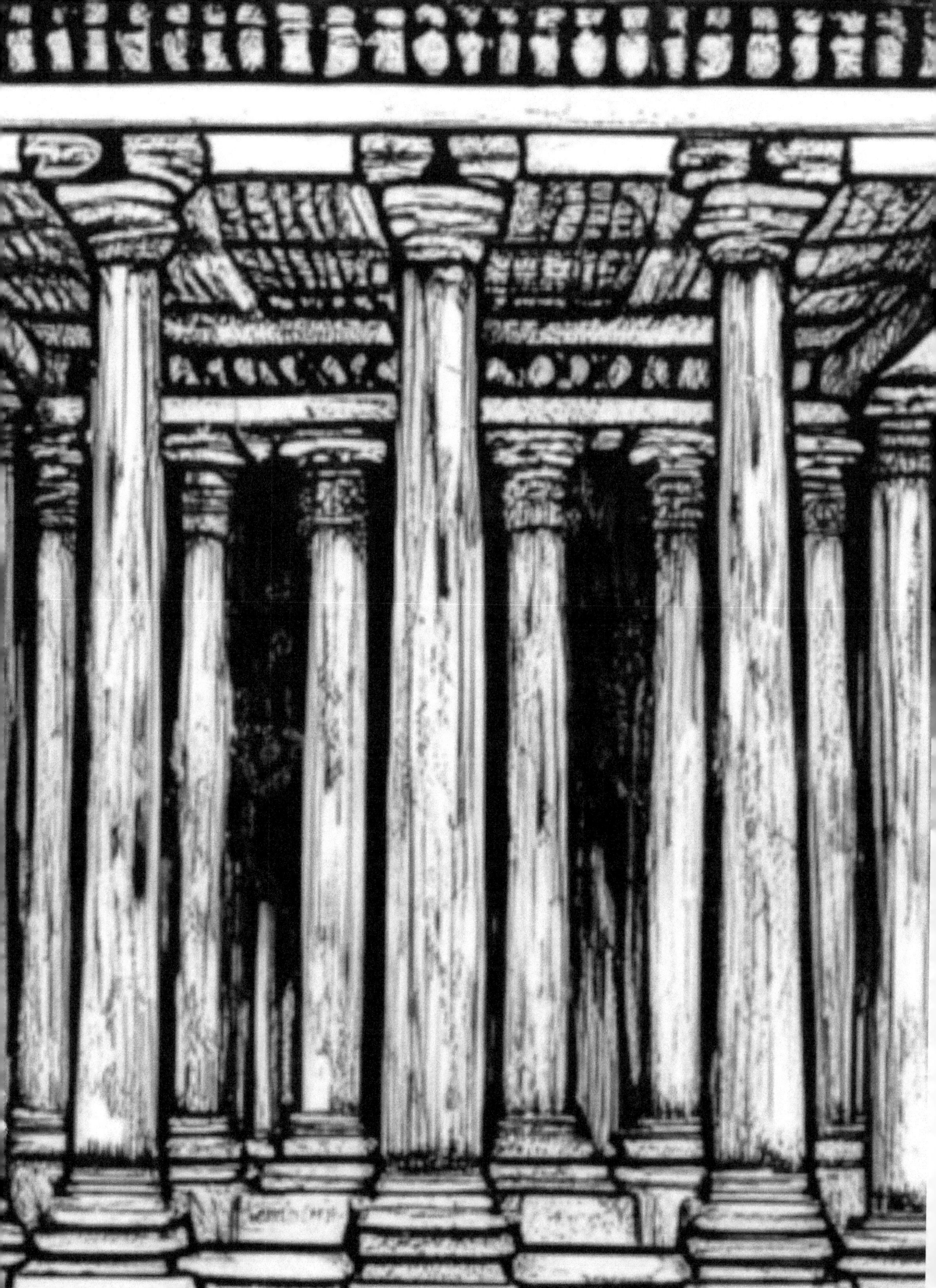

THANK YOU FOR BUYING MY BOOK.
I HOPE YOU ENJOY IT!

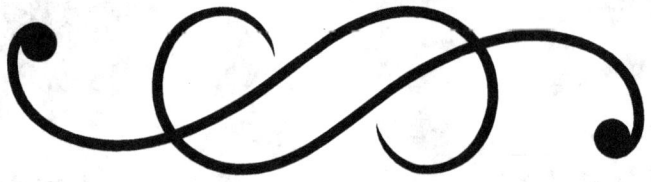

Rebecca Rae